HOW TO START AND GROW A SUCCESSFUL BUSINESS

Turn Your Business Dreams into a Successful Venture

Brandon L. Kennedy

TABLE OF CONTENT

Foreword

Every great journey begins with a single step, and every remarkable achievement starts with a vision. In the world of entrepreneurship, this journey can be likened to setting sail on uncharted seas. The voyage is both exhilarating and challenging, filled with moments of discovery, innovation, and resilience.

As I embark on the privilege of penning this foreword for " how to start and grow a successful business" I am reminded of the countless entrepreneurs I've met throughout my career. Each one possessed a unique story, a distinct vision, and an unyielding determination to chart their course to success. Their journeys, much like those of the pioneers and explorers of old, have left indelible marks on industries, economies, and societies.

What sets this book apart is its commitment to providing not just theoretical knowledge but practical wisdom—a compass for entrepreneurs to navigate the entrepreneurial seas with purpose and precision. The author has distilled a wealth of experience and expertise into these pages, offering a comprehensive guide that spans the entire entrepreneurial landscape.

As you delve into the chapters that follows, you will encounter strategic insights, real-world examples, and actionable advice that can empower you to make informed decisions. You will explore the importance of location and infrastructure, gain a deep understanding of branding and marketing, and learn the art of customer acquisition, sales distribution, and financial management.

But this book is not just about strategy; it's about cultivating an entrepreneurial spirit—an indomitable force that propels you forward, no matter the challenges you encounter. It encourages you to embrace innovation, adaptability, and a relentless pursuit of excellence. It invites you to turn adversity into opportunity, to build meaningful relationships, and to leave a lasting legacy.

Entrepreneurship is more than a career; it's a way of life. It requires not only knowledge and skill but also character and resilience. It demands the courage to set sail into uncharted waters, the creativity to navigate obstacles, and the wisdom to seize opportunities. " How to Start and Grow a Successful Business" equips you with the tools to embark on this remarkable journey with confidence.

May your entrepreneurial odyssey be marked by courage, innovation, and unwavering determination

Fair winds and following seas.

By Carmella T. McGill

INTRODUCTION

Welcome aboard the extraordinary journey of entrepreneurship—a voyage where dreams are transformed into reality, challenges are met with unwavering determination, and success is navigated by the compass of innovation. Get ready to embark on an adventure like no other with "How to start and grow a successful business."

Imagine standing at the helm of your own ship, charting a course through uncharted waters, and discovering new horizons of opportunity. This book is your compass, your guiding star, and your trusted first mate as you navigate the dynamic landscape of entrepreneurship.

Setting Sail for Excellence: Whether you're a budding entrepreneur with a brilliant idea or a seasoned business leader seeking fresh strategies, this book is designed to be your ultimate toolkit. From mastering the art of visionary planning to conquering the high seas of scaling and growth, you'll embark on a transformative journey that will shape your entrepreneurial destiny.

Venture Beyond the Horizon: Dive into the world of strategic planning, where every decision is a ripple that shapes your business's trajectory. Learn the art of calculated risk-taking, create business plans that defy the ordinary, and set sail with a vision that propels you beyond the horizon.

Navigating Challenges with Finesse: Just as intrepid explorers navigate treacherous waters, entrepreneurs must navigate challenges with resilience and adaptability. Discover the secrets of turning setbacks into stepping stones and learn how to steer your ship even in the face of stormy seas.

Unlocking the Power of Partnerships: In the ever-evolving world of business, partnerships are the winds that fill your sails and propel you forward. Uncover the strategies for forging alliances, building connections, and harnessing the power of collaboration that can take your ventures to new heights.

Embrace Your Inner Navigator: Beyond strategies and plans, this book is about fostering an entrepreneurial spirit that's unafraid to venture where others hesitate. It's about nurturing a mindset that thrives on challenges and converts setbacks into opportunities. It's about unleashing your inner navigator—the force that propels you towards the shores of success.

Set Your Course for Triumph: Are you ready to seize the helm, steer your ship, and navigate the entrepreneurial odyssey with confidence? This book is your compass, your guide, and your beacon of light as you sail through uncharted waters. So, hoist your sails, set your course for triumph, and let this book be your constant companion on this exhilarating voyage.

Embrace the adventure. Grab your copy, and let's set sail together on a journey that promises transformation, innovation, and unparalleled success.

CHAPTER ONE
Idea Generation and Market Research

The inception of a successful business marks the realization of an idea—an idea that germinates from a combination of personal passion, experience, observation, and the recognition of an unmet need in the market.

The journey of entrepreneurship begins with this foundational step: idea generation. However, mere idea generation isn't enough to guarantee success; it must be nurtured by a comprehensive process of market research to ensure viability, relevance, and potential for growth.

Idea Generation: The Creative Nexus

Idea generation is the crucible where creativity, personal strengths, and entrepreneurial vision converge.

It's not simply about brainstorming, but a structured process of self-discovery and identification of opportunities.

The process begins by introspecting—understanding one's own skills, passions, and experiences. What are you genuinely enthusiastic about? What skills and expertise do you possess that could translate into a valuable offering?

The synergy between personal passion and market demand is pivotal. An idea that aligns with your strengths and passions is more likely to sustain your enthusiasm through the challenging phases of business development. This intrinsic motivation becomes the driving force behind your commitment and perseverance.

Furthermore, great ideas often spring from recognizing problems or inefficiencies in your daily life or industry. By paying attention to pain points and gaps, you can uncover opportunities for innovative solutions.

Consider the story of many successful startups—Uber identified the need for convenient transportation, Airbnb leveraged unused living spaces, and Dropbox simplified file sharing. Each of these ideas was rooted in addressing real-world challenges.

Market Research: Illuminating the Path Forward

Once an idea takes root, it's time to subject it to the litmus test of market research. This phase is about seeking validation, understanding your target audience, and gaining insights into the competitive landscape. Market research transforms a fledgling idea into a well-informed business concept.

Understanding the needs of your potential customers: Your idea might be compelling, but is there a demand for it? Who are your potential customers? What are the values they crave, their behaviors, and their pain points? By delving into demographics, psychographics, and behavioral patterns, you can tailor your idea to suit the needs of your intended audience.

Analyzing Competition: Every business operates within a competitive ecosystem. Identifying existing players in your chosen domain helps you understand market dynamics, spot gaps, and differentiate your offering. This analysis provides a foundation for developing a unique value proposition that sets your business apart.

Industry Trends and Forecasting: Successful entrepreneurs are not just focused on the present; they anticipate future trends. Through market research, you can identify emerging trends, technological advancements, and shifts in consumer behavior. This foresight enables you to position your business ahead of the curve.

Primary and Secondary Research: Effective market research involves a blend of primary and secondary research. Primary research normally involves direct interaction with potential customers through surveys, focus groups, or interviews. This provides nuanced insights into their needs and preferences. Secondary research involves gathering data from existing sources like industry reports, articles, and online databases.

The Symbiotic Relationship Between Idea and Research: The relationship between idea generation and market research is symbiotic. An idea that is solely driven by personal passion, without considering market demand, can lead to a misalignment between the product/service and the consumer's needs.

Conversely, conducting market research without a creative and original idea can result in a business that lacks innovation and fails to captivate the market.

A successful business idea is one that bridges the gap between personal enthusiasm and market demand. It's an idea that not only resonates with you but also provides value to customers. This harmony ensures that your business isn't just a fleeting trend but has the potential for longevity and growth.

Innovation and Adaptation: The Ongoing Journey

The process of idea generation and market research is not confined to the early stages of entrepreneurship. It's a continuous journey that evolves as your business grows and the market changes.

As you gain more insights from customer feedback, adapt to technological advancements, and respond to shifts in demand, you might find opportunities to refine your initial idea or pivot in a new direction.

In conclusion, idea generation and market research are the foundational pillars of a successful business venture. An innovative idea nurtured by thorough research not only ensures the viability of your business but also positions it for growth and resilience.

This process demands a delicate balance of creativity and analytical rigor—a dance between passion and pragmatism. By embracing this journey with an open mind and a willingness to learn, you set the stage for a business that not only succeeds but also leaves a lasting impact on the market.

CHAPTER TWO
Business Plan

In the realm of entrepreneurship, a business plan is more than a mere document; it's a strategic blueprint that guides every facet of your venture.

A well-crafted business plan encapsulates your vision, outlines your strategies, anticipates challenges, and charts a clear path toward achieving your goals. It's the cornerstone of informed decision-making and serves as a roadmap for success.

Let's delve into the intricacies of creating a comprehensive business plan that not only secures funding but also lays the foundation for sustainable growth.

The Essence of a Business Plan

At its core, a business plan is a structured narrative that communicates your business idea, its potential, and the strategies you'll employ to transform that potential into reality. Think of it as the story of your business, with each section contributing to a cohesive and compelling narrative.

1. Business Description: Painting the Picture

This section is an expansion of the executive summary, providing a deeper dive into the core elements of your business. It outlines the nature of your business, its mission and vision, the problem it addresses, and the solution it offers. It's an opportunity to communicate your passion for the venture and your understanding of the market gap you aim to fill. Be sure to highlight what sets your business apart and your long-term goals for growth.

2. Market Analysis: Navigating the Landscape

Market analysis is the compass that guides your business plan. It involves a comprehensive examination of your target market, industry trends, customer needs, and competitive landscape. Delve into market size, segmentation, and growth potential. Identify your ideal customer persona and explore their preferences, behaviors, and pain points. A robust market analysis demonstrates a profound understanding of the environment in which your business will operate.

3. Competitive Analysis: Mapping the Terrain

Understanding your competition is as critical as knowing your customers. A competitive analysis delves into the strengths and weaknesses of existing players in your industry. Identify direct and indirect competitors, and analyze their products/services, pricing strategies, distribution channels, and market positioning. This analysis helps you carve out a unique value proposition and identify opportunities to differentiate your business.

4. Marketing and Sales Strategy: Forging Connections

Your business may have a brilliant product or service, but without effective marketing and sales strategies, its potential may remain untapped. Describe how you'll reach your target audience through branding, advertising, public relations, and digital marketing. Outline your sales approach, distribution channels, and customer acquisition tactics. A well-defined marketing and sales strategy ensures your business connects with customers and drives revenue.

5. Product/Service Line: Crafting Excellence

In this section, you give a detailed description of your products or services. Highlight their features, benefits, and how they address customer needs. If applicable, discuss your product development process, intellectual property, and any competitive advantages you hold. Focus on how your offerings meet market demands and provide unique solutions.

6. Operational Plan: The Engine of Efficiency

The operational plan defines how your business will operate on a day-to-day basis. It covers areas such as production, supply chain management, quality control, facilities, technology infrastructure, and staffing requirements. This section demonstrates your ability to execute your business strategies and maintain operational efficiency.

7. Financial Projections: Predicting the Future

Financial projections provide a glimpse into the financial viability of your business. Include detailed revenue forecasts, expense estimates, profit margins, and cash flow projections. This section is a testament to your financial acumen and demonstrates your understanding of the financial resources required to sustain and grow your business.

8. Funding Request: Fueling Growth

If you're seeking funding, this section outlines your capital requirements and how you intend to use the funds. Specify the amount of funding needed, the purpose it will serve (e.g., product development, marketing, expansion), and the anticipated returns for investors. This section should align with your financial projections and present a compelling case for investment.

9. Team and Management: The Human Backbone

Investors don't simply invest in ideas; they also invest in the people who create them. Introduce your management team and key personnel, highlighting their relevant experience, skills, and contributions to the business. Showcase the strengths that make your team well-equipped to execute the business plan effectively.

10. Implementation Timeline: Turning Plans into Action

A business plan without a timeline is just a set of aspirations. Create a timeline that outlines the key milestones and deadlines for your business's development. This timeline not only keeps your team accountable but also shows potential investors that you have a clear plan for execution.

11. Risks and Mitigation Strategies: Navigating Uncertainty

Every business faces risks. Acknowledge potential challenges that could affect your business's success, whether they're related to market fluctuations, regulatory changes, or operational disruptions. Develop strategies to mitigate these risks and showcase your readiness to adapt and overcome them.

12. Exit Strategy: The End Game

An exit strategy outlines your plan for the future, whether it involves selling the business, merging with another company, or going public. While this might seem premature, having an exit strategy shows that you're forward-thinking and strategic in your approach.

Beyond Words on Paper

In essence, a business plan is not a static document but a living, breathing roadmap that guides your entrepreneurial journey. Crafting a comprehensive business plan demands a blend of creativity, analytical rigor, and strategic thinking. Each section is a brushstroke in the portrait of your business, coming together to create a vivid and compelling image of what your venture could become.

Remember that the process of creating a business plan is not an isolated exercise. It's an opportunity for introspection, research, and refinement. As your business evolves, your plan should evolve with it.

A well-structured business plan doesn't just attract investors; it empowers you to make informed decisions, adapt to changing circumstances, and navigate the dynamic landscape of entrepreneurship with confidence.

CHAPTER THREE
Legal Formalities

In the complex and multifaceted world of entrepreneurship, navigating the legal landscape is not just a necessity; it's a critical component of building a successful business.

The process of establishing a solid legal foundation for your enterprise encompasses various aspects, from selecting the appropriate legal structure to obtaining licenses and permits, protecting intellectual property, and ensuring compliance with local, state, and federal regulations.

This comprehensive exploration delves into the intricacies of legal formalities and their pivotal role in the journey to business success.

1. Selecting the Right Legal Structure: Setting the Business's DNA

Choosing the right legal structure for your business is akin to selecting its DNA. This decision profoundly influences how your business operates, is taxed, and manages liability. The legal structure options available to entrepreneurs generally include sole proprietorships, partnerships, limited liability companies (LLCs), corporations, and various hybrids. Each structure has its advantages and disadvantages, so it's crucial to assess which one aligns best with your business goals and circumstances.

a. Sole Proprietorship: This is the simplest and most common form of business ownership. In a sole proprietorship, you are the business's sole owner and operator. While this structure offers complete control, it also means you're personally liable for the business's debts and obligations.

b. Partnership: Partnerships involve two or more individuals who share ownership and responsibility for the business. Partnerships can be general (where all partners share in profits and losses) or limited (where some partners have limited liability). Like sole proprietorships, partnerships expose owners to personal liability.

c. Limited Liability Company (LLC): An LLC offers the flexibility of a partnership while providing limited liability protection for owners (members). This means members' personal assets are typically shielded from business debts and lawsuits. LLCs are a common choice for small businesses.

d. Corporation: Corporations are distinct legal entities separate from their owners (shareholders). They offer the strongest liability protection but involve more complex regulations and formalities. Corporations can be S corporations (pass-through taxation) or C corporations (double taxation).

e. Hybrid Structures: Some businesses opt for hybrid structures, such as S corporations or limited liability partnerships (LLPs), to combine elements of different legal forms.

Choosing the Right Structure: A Balancing Act

The choice of legal structure depends on several factors, including your business's size, industry, financing needs, and your long-term goals. It's not a one-size-fits-all decision.

Liability Protection: If you're concerned about personal liability for business debts or legal issues, structures like LLCs or corporations offer greater protection.

Taxation: Consider how the business's income will be taxed. Some structures, like sole proprietorships and partnerships, allow for pass-through taxation, where business profits are reported on the owners' individual tax returns.

Corporations may face double taxation, with income taxed at the corporate level and then again when distributed as dividends.

Complexity and Regulations: Different structures come with varying degrees of complexity and regulatory requirements.

Sole proprietorships and partnerships are relatively simple, while corporations entail more formalities.

Ownership and Control: Evaluate how you want to manage ownership and control. Partnerships allow shared decision-making, while corporations often have boards of directors and shareholders.

Funding and Investment: Consider how you plan to raise capital. Corporations, for instance, can issue stocks, making them attractive to investors.

Exit Strategy: Think about your long-term plans for the business.

If you anticipate going public or selling the company, a corporate structure may be more suitable.

2. Registering Your Business: The Legal Birth Certificate

Once you've determined the appropriate legal structure, the next step is to formally register your business with the relevant authorities. This process provides your business with a legal identity and ensures that it complies with local, state, and fedcral regulations. Registration requirements can vary depending on your location and business type, but typically involve the following steps:

a. Choose a Business Name: Select a unique and legally compliant name for your business. Ensure it's not already in use by another entity in your state.

b. Register with the Appropriate Authorities: Depending on your legal structure, you may need to register with various government agencies. For example, you might need to file articles of organization with the state for an LLC or articles of incorporation for a corporation.

c. Obtain an Employer Identification Number (EIN): An EIN, also known as a federal tax identification number, is essential for tax reporting and hiring employees. You can obtain one from the IRS.

d. Comply with Local Regulations: Check with your local government to ensure you comply with zoning laws, licensing requirements, and other local regulations.

e. Register for State Taxes: If your state imposes sales tax or income tax, you may need to register for these taxes and obtain the necessary permits.

f. Apply for Business Licenses and Permits: Depending on your industry and location, you may need specific licenses or permits to operate legally. Examples include a liquor license for a restaurant or a health permit for a food service business.

3. Intellectual Property Protection: Safeguarding Your Ideas

In the knowledge-based economy of today, intellectual property (IP) can be as valuable as physical assets. Protecting your IP ensures that your ideas, inventions, and creative works are safeguarded from unauthorized use or replication. IP can take many forms, including patents, copyrights trademarks, and trade secrets. Here's a closer look at each:

a. Patents: Patents protect inventions, giving the holder exclusive rights to make, use, and sell the invention for a specified period (usually 20 years). To obtain a patent, you must file an application with the United States Patent and Trademark Office (USPTO) and demonstrate that your invention is novel, non-obvious, and useful.

b. Trademarks: Trademarks protect brand names, logos, and symbols that distinguish your products or services from others in the market. Registering a trademark with the USPTO provides legal protection and the exclusive right to use that mark in commerce.

c. Copyrights: Copyrights protect original works of authorship, including literature, music, art, and software. Unlike patents and trademarks, copyrights are automatically granted upon the creation of the work. However, registering your copyright with the U.S. Copyright Office provides additional legal benefits.

d. Trade Secrets: Trade secrets encompass confidential business information that provides a competitive advantage. This can include formulas, processes, customer lists, and marketing strategies. To protect trade secrets, businesses often use non-disclosure agreements (NDAs) and implement strict internal security measures.

The Role of Intellectual Property in Business

Intellectual property is integral to protecting your business's innovations and competitive edge. It can:

Deter Competitors: Having a patent, trademark, or copyright signals to competitors that you take IP seriously and are willing to defend your rights.

Enhance Brand Value: Trademarks can increase the value of your brand, making it more appealing to customers and potential investors.

Generate Revenue: You can monetize IP by licensing it to others or selling it outright.

Facilitate Investment: Investors may be more willing to fund your business if they see that you have protected your valuable IP.

4. Contracts and Agreements: The Legal Framework of Business

Contracts and agreements serve as the legal framework of your business relationships. They formalize commitments, outline expectations, and protect the interests of all parties involved. Here's a look at some essential contracts and agreements that are fundamental to your business's legal health:

a. Operating Agreements: For LLCs, an operating agreement outlines the structure of the company, ownership percentages, voting rights, profit distribution, and procedures for decision-making.

b. Partnership Agreements: Partnerships should have a clear partnership agreement that defines each partner's roles, responsibilities, and the terms of the partnership.

c. Shareholder Agreements: In corporations, shareholder agreements specify the rights and obligations of shareholders, including matters related to share transfer, management, and dispute resolution.

d. Employment Contracts: Employment contracts outline the terms and conditions of employment for your staff. They clarify roles, responsibilities, compensation, benefits, and other important details.

e. Vendor and Supplier Contracts: Contracts with vendors and suppliers outline the terms of purchase, delivery, pricing, and quality standards. Clear agreements can prevent misunderstandings and disputes.

f. Client Agreements: When providing products or services to clients, client agreements establish expectations, deliverables, payment terms, and deadlines.

g. Non-Disclosure Agreements (NDAs): NDAs protect sensitive information when sharing it with employees, partners, contractors, or potential collaborators.

h. Licensing Agreements: If you're licensing your intellectual property to others, such as software or copyrighted content, licensing agreements specify the terms and conditions of use.

i. Lease Agreements: If you're leasing a physical location for your business, a lease agreement outlines the terms of the lease, including rent, duration, and maintenance responsibilities.

j. Non-Compete and Non-Solicitation Agreements: These agreements prevent employees, contractors, or business partners from competing with your business or soliciting your clients or employees.

Why Contracts Matter

Contracts and agreements set clear expectations and prevent misunderstandings. They provide legal recourse in case of disputes and ensure that all parties involved are on the same page. A well-drafted contract can protect your interests, save you time and money, and contribute to the overall stability of your business.

5. Compliance with Regulations: Navigating the Legal Maze

Compliance with regulations is not just a legal obligation; it's a foundational principle of ethical and responsible business conduct. Governments at various levels establish rules and regulations to ensure public safety, fair competition, and ethical business practices. Complying with these regulations demonstrates your commitment to transparency and accountability. Key areas of regulatory compliance include:

a. Tax Compliance: Businesses must adhere to federal, state, and local tax regulations. This includes filing accurate tax returns, remitting taxes on time, and keeping proper records.

b. Employment Laws: Employment laws govern various aspects of the employer-employee relationship, including minimum wage, overtime, workplace safety, anti-discrimination, and employee benefits.

c. Health and Safety Regulations: Depending on your industry, you may need to comply with health and safety regulations to ensure the well-being of your employees and customers.

d. Environmental Regulations: Businesses involved in manufacturing, construction, or other activities with potential environmental impact must comply with environmental regulations.

e. Data Privacy and Security: If your business collects and stores customer data, you must adhere to data privacy laws and implement security measures to protect sensitive information.

f. Industry-Specific Regulations: Certain industries, such as healthcare, finance, and food service, have specialized regulations that businesses must comply with.

g. Licensing and Permits: Depending on your location and industry, you may need specific licenses or permits to operate legally. Failure to obtain the necessary permits can lead to fines or closure.

h. Accessibility Requirements: Digital businesses should ensure their websites and online content comply with accessibility standards to accommodate individuals with disabilities.

The Consequences of Non-Compliance

Non-compliance with regulations can lead to severe consequences, including legal penalties, fines, lawsuits, damage to reputation, and even business closure. It's essential to stay informed about relevant regulations, continuously monitor changes, and establish processes to ensure ongoing compliance.

The Legal Tapestry of Business

Building a business without addressing legal formalities is like constructing a house without a solid foundation. Legal considerations are interwoven throughout every stage of entrepreneurship, from inception to growth.

Selecting the right legal structure, registering your business, protecting intellectual property, drafting contracts, and ensuring regulatory compliance collectively create a legal tapestry that supports the growth and sustainability of your enterprise.

While the legal landscape may seem daunting, it's not a path you need to navigate alone. Legal professionals, such as attorneys and business consultants, can provide guidance tailored to your specific circumstances.

Embracing legal formalities isn't just about meeting legal requirements—it's about creating an environment where your business can thrive with confidence, knowing that its legal foundation is strong and secure.

By weaving legal considerations into the fabric of your business strategy, you're not only safeguarding your venture but also positioning it for success in a complex and ever-evolving business world.

CHAPTER FOUR
Finances

In the dynamic world of entrepreneurship, mastering financial management is akin to sailing a ship through turbulent waters.

Just as a skilled captain navigates the seas to reach their destination, a savvy entrepreneur must navigate the complexities of business finances to steer their venture toward success.

From understanding startup costs to managing cash flow, securing funding, and making strategic financial decisions, this exploration delves into the intricacies of financial management and its role in building a thriving business.

1. Understanding Startup Costs: Laying the Financial Foundation

Every successful venture begins with a solid understanding of its financial landscape. Startup costs encompass all the expenses associated with launching your business, from product development and equipment purchase to marketing and office space.

An accurate assessment of startup costs is critical for budgeting, securing funding, and setting realistic expectations. Here's a breakdown of key startup cost categories:

a. One-time Costs: These include expenses that occur only at the beginning, such as equipment purchases, initial inventory, legal and licensing fees, website development, and branding.

b. Recurring Costs: Recurring costs are ongoing operational expenses that you'll need to cover regularly. These can include rent, utilities, salaries, insurance, marketing expenses, and software subscriptions.

c. Marketing and Sales: Building brand awareness and acquiring customers requires an investment in marketing and sales efforts. This can include advertising, social media campaigns, website optimization, and sales team salaries.

d. Research and Development: If your business involves product development or innovation, allocate funds for research, prototyping, and testing.

e. Contingency Fund: It's wise to set aside a contingency fund for unexpected expenses or business fluctuations.

2. Budgeting and Financial Planning: Charting Your Course

Budgeting is the compass that guides your financial journey. A well-structured budget provides a roadmap for allocating resources, tracking expenses, and assessing financial health. It helps you make informed decisions, avoid overspending, and ensure you have the capital needed to grow and adapt. Creating a budget involves several steps:

a. Identify Income Sources: Estimate your sources of income, including sales revenue, investment capital, and any other funding.

b. List Expenses: Categorize your expenses into fixed costs (consistent month to month) and variable costs (fluctuate based on business activity).

c. Set Priorities: Determine which expenses are critical for your business's operations and growth. Allocate resources accordingly.

d. Monitor and Adjust: Regularly review your budget and compare actual expenses with projected ones. To keep on track, make adjustments as needed.

3. Cash Flow Management: Sailing Smoothly or Weathering Storms

Cash flow—the movement of money in and out of your business—is the lifeblood of any enterprise. Even a profitable business can face challenges if cash flow isn't managed effectively.

Positive cash flow ensures you have enough funds to cover expenses, invest in growth, and weather unforeseen challenges. Here are strategies for effective cash flow management:

a. Monitor Inflows and Outflows: Keep a close eye on the timing of revenue collection and payment of expenses. Delays in either can disrupt cash flow.

b. Project Future Cash Flow: Use historical data to forecast future cash flow. This allows you to plan ahead of time for anticipated deficits.

c. Implement Credit Policies: If your business extends credit to customers, establish clear credit policies to minimize late payments and improve cash flow.

d. Manage Inventory: Overstocking can tie up funds, while understocking can lead to missed sales. Balance inventory levels to optimize cash flow.

e. Control Expenses: Regularly review expenses to identify areas where you can cut costs without sacrificing quality.

4. Funding Your Business: The Capital Infusion

For many entrepreneurs, securing funding is a critical step in getting their business off the ground or fueling its growth. While some businesses can be bootstrapped using personal savings, others require external capital. Funding options include:

a. Personal Savings: Using your own savings to fund the business is a common approach. It offers control and avoids taking on debt or giving up equity.

b. Family and Friends: Borrowing from friends and family can be a source of early-stage capital. However, clear terms and communication are essential to prevent strained relationships.

c. Bank Loans: Traditional bank loans are a common funding option. They provide a lump sum of money that is repaid with interest over time.

d. Angel Investors: Angel investors are individuals who invest their personal funds in startups in exchange for equity. They often provide mentorship and connections along with capital.

e. Venture Capital: Venture capitalists (VCs) invest in high-growth startups in exchange for equity. They often provide larger sums of money to fuel rapid expansion.

f. Crowdfunding: Online platforms allow you to raise small amounts of money from a large number of people. This can be a way to validate your idea and gain early customers.

g. Grants and Competitions: Some businesses are eligible for grants, particularly those in certain industries or pursuing socially beneficial goals. Competitions can also provide funding as prizes.

h. Bootstrapping: Bootstrapping involves using minimal external funding and relying on revenue generated by the business to support growth.

5. Financial Decision-Making: Plotting the Course to Profit

Effective financial decision-making is at the heart of business success. It involves analyzing data, evaluating risks and rewards, and making choices that align with your business goals. Here are key areas where financial decisions play a crucial role:

a. Pricing Strategy: Determine how to price your products or services to cover costs, generate profit, and remain competitive in the market.

b. Capital Expenditures: Decisions about investing in long-term assets such as equipment, technology, or facilities impact your business's efficiency and growth.

c. Expansion: Assess the financial feasibility and potential returns of expanding to new markets, opening additional locations, or launching new product lines.

d. Debt Management: If you've taken on debt, managing repayments and interest costs is essential to avoid financial strain.

e. Investment in Growth: Decide how much of your profits to reinvest in the business for growth versus distributing as profits.

f. Risk Management: Evaluate risks to your business, such as market changes, competition, and economic downturns. Develop strategies to mitigate these risks.

6. Financial Reporting and Analysis: Navigating by the Numbers

Financial reporting provides the map by which you navigate your business's performance. Regularly analyzing financial statements allows you to assess profitability, track trends, and make informed decisions. Key financial statements include:

a. Income Statement (Profit and Loss): This statement shows your revenue, expenses, and net profit or loss over a specific period. It's a snapshot of your business's financial performance.

b. Balance Sheet: The balance sheet provides a snapshot of your business's financial position at a specific point in time. It lists assets, liabilities, and equity.

c. Cash Flow Statement: This statement tracks the inflow and outflow of cash from operating, investing, and financing activities.

d. Financial Ratios: Ratios like profitability, liquidity, and efficiency ratios help you assess your business's financial health and compare it to industry benchmarks.

e. Trend Analysis: Comparing financial data over time helps identify patterns, shifts, and potential areas for improvement.

7. Financial Technology and Tools: The Modern Navigation Aids

In today's digital age, financial technology (FinTech) tools can significantly streamline financial management. From accounting software and apps to payment platforms budgeting and financial analytics tools, there's an array of resources available to entrepreneurs.

These tools can automate processes, provide real-time insights, and improve accuracy in financial reporting and analysis.

The Compass to Business Success

Navigating the financial aspects of entrepreneurship is both an art and a science. Just as a captain relies on navigation tools, charts, and experience to guide a ship, an entrepreneur relies on financial management principles, data analysis, and strategic decision-making to steer their business toward success.

Understanding startup costs, budgeting, managing cash flow, securing funding, and making informed financial decisions are all critical components of this voyage.

Financial acumen empowers entrepreneurs to make confident choices, adapt to challenges, and seize opportunities for growth. It's not just about balancing the books; it's about steering the ship with a steady hand, charting a course to profitability, sustainability, and lasting success.

By mastering the financial seas, entrepreneurs can ensure their businesses not only stay afloat but thrive in the dynamic and ever-evolving landscape of entrepreneurship.

CHAPTER FIVE
Location and Infrastructure

In the ever-evolving world of entrepreneurship, the adage "Location, location, location" still holds immense significance. The choice of where to establish your business and the quality of the infrastructure supporting it can greatly influence your chances of success.

This exploration delves into the multifaceted realm of location and infrastructure in entrepreneurship, unveiling the critical factors, strategic considerations, and practical steps that underpin these cornerstones of business achievement.

1. Location Matters: The Art and Science of Site Selection

Selecting the right location for your business is akin to choosing the ideal soil for planting a seed. It sets the stage for growth, determines the available resources, and significantly impacts the business's long-term prospects. Here's a closer look at why location matters:

a. Accessibility: A prime location should be easily accessible to your target audience, whether they are customers, clients, or partners. Consider proximity to transportation hubs, major roads, and public transit.

b. Demographics: The demographic profile of the area can influence the demand for your products or services. Analyze factors such as population size, income levels, age groups, and cultural diversity.

c. Competition: Assess the competitive landscape in your chosen location. Consider the number and strength of competitors, as well as their market share.

d. Regulations: Different regions have varying regulatory environments. Investigate local laws, taxes, permits, and licensing requirements that may impact your business operations.

e. Costs: The cost of operating in a particular location can significantly affect your bottom line. Evaluate expenses such as rent, utilities, labor, and taxes.

f. Infrastructure: Examine the quality of infrastructure, including utilities, telecommunications, and internet connectivity. Reliable infrastructure is essential for efficient operations.

g. Talent Pool: Consider the availability of a skilled workforce in the area. A talented and educated labor pool can be a valuable asset to your business.

h. Market Research: Conduct thorough market research to understand consumer behavior, preferences, and trends in the chosen location. This knowledge will inform your business strategy.

i. Future Growth: Anticipate the future growth potential of the area. A location that is poised for development may offer opportunities for long-term expansion.

j. Sustainability: In today's environmentally conscious world, consider the sustainability of your chosen location. Green infrastructure and sustainable practices can enhance your brand's reputation.

k. Risk Assessment: Evaluate potential risks associated with the location, such as natural disasters, political instability, or economic volatility. Develop contingency plans to mitigate these risks.

2. Strategies for Effective Site Selection: Navigating the Business Landscape

Selecting the right location involves a mix of data-driven analysis and strategic thinking. Just as skilled navigators chart their course with precision, entrepreneurs must navigate the business landscape to choose the optimal site. Here are key strategies for effective site selection:

a. Define Your Criteria: Begin by defining clear criteria for your ideal location. Consider factors like target market, industry ecosystem, and growth potential.

b. Conduct Market Research: Gather comprehensive market data to understand consumer behavior, market trends, and competition in the chosen area.

c. Site Visits: Visit potential locations in person to assess their suitability. Take note of traffic patterns, accessibility, and the overall environment.

d. Competitive Analysis: Analyze the competitive landscape in the area. Identify key competitors, their strengths, weaknesses, and market positioning.

e. Cost-Benefit Analysis: Conduct a thorough cost-benefit analysis to compare the expenses associated with different locations. Consider both short-term and long-term costs.

f. Regulatory Compliance: Ensure that you understand and can comply with all local regulations, permits, and licensing requirements. Seek legal counsel if necessary.

g. Infrastructure Evaluation: Assess the quality and reliability of infrastructure in the area. Reliable utilities and communication systems are vital for business operations.

h. Workforce Availability: Research the availability of skilled labor in the region. Evaluate local universities and institutions as potential sources of talent.

i. Network and Relationships: Leverage your network and industry relationships for insights into the suitability of specific locations. Connect with local business associations and chambers of commerce.

j. Test the Market: Consider conducting a soft launch or pilot program in the area to gauge market response and fine-tune your business model.

k. Future Projections: Explore economic and demographic forecasts for the region. A location with anticipated growth can offer opportunities for expansion.

l.   Environmental   Impact: Assess   the environmental impact of your business operations. Consider adopting sustainable practices that align with the location's values.

m. Risk Mitigation: Develop a risk mitigation plan that addresses potential challenges associated with the chosen location. This plan should include contingencies for various scenarios.

3. Location Case Study: Silicon Valley's Innovation Ecosystem

One of the most iconic examples of the impact of location on business success is Silicon Valley. Nestled in the southern part of the San Francisco Bay Area in California, Silicon Valley has earned its reputation as the global hub of technology and innovation. What makes this region so special?

a. Proximity to Talent: Silicon Valley is home to some of the world's most prestigious universities and research institutions, including Stanford University and UC Berkeley. This concentration of intellectual capital attracts top talent from around the world.

b. Venture Capital Hub: The region boasts an extensive network of venture capital firms and angel investors willing to fund innovative startups. Access to capital is crucial for scaling businesses.

c. Industry Ecosystem: A dense ecosystem of tech giants, startups, incubators, accelerators, and research labs fosters collaboration, knowledge sharing, and innovation.

d. Culture of Risk-Taking: Silicon Valley's culture encourages risk-taking and embraces failure as a stepping stone to success. This mindset fuels entrepreneurship.

e. Supportive Infrastructure: The area offers state-of-the-art infrastructure, including reliable internet connectivity, transportation, and utilities.

f. Networking Opportunities: Networking events, conferences, and meetups are plentiful, providing entrepreneurs with opportunities to connect with like-minded individuals.

g. Prestige and Branding: The Silicon Valley brand carries prestige and credibility, attracting both customers and investors.

h. Innovation Ecosystem: The region is at the forefront of technological advancements, making it an ideal location for businesses at the cutting edge of innovation.

i. Global Reach: Silicon Valley's proximity to major international airports facilitates global business expansion.

4. Infrastructure: Building Blocks for Business Success

Infrastructure is the backbone of business operations. It encompasses physical and virtual elements that support the smooth functioning of your enterprise. Just as navigators rely on sturdy ships, entrepreneurs depend on reliable infrastructure to navigate the challenges of the business world. Here's a breakdown of the essential components of business infrastructure:

a. Physical Infrastructure: This includes tangible assets such as office space, manufacturing facilities, warehouses, and transportation systems. The quality and efficiency of these assets impact your ability to deliver products and services.

b. Digital Infrastructure: In the digital age, robust digital infrastructure is paramount. It encompasses hardware, software, data centers, cloud services, and cybersecurity measures. A secure and efficient digital infrastructure ensures seamless communication, data management, and online presence.

c. Supply Chain Infrastructure: A well-structured supply chain is vital for businesses involved in manufacturing and distribution. It includes sourcing raw materials, inventory management, production processes, and logistics.

d. Communication Infrastructure: Effective communication is central to business operations. Reliable phone systems, email services, video conferencing platforms, and collaboration tools facilitate internal and external communication.

e. Energy and Utilities: Access to a stable and affordable supply of energy and utilities (electricity, water, gas) is essential for uninterrupted operations.

f. Transportation and Logistics: Efficient transportation systems and logistics networks enable the movement of goods and services. Consider the proximity of suppliers, customers, and distribution channels when evaluating infrastructure.

g. Regulatory Compliance: Infrastructure should align with regulatory standards and compliance requirements specific to your industry and location.

h. Scalability: Infrastructure should be scalable to accommodate business growth. As your operations expand, the infrastructure should adapt to increased demand.

i. Disaster Recovery and Redundancy: Implementing disaster recovery plans and redundancy measures ensures business continuity in the event of unexpected disruptions.

j. Sustainability: Increasingly, businesses are incorporating sustainability into their infrastructure. Green building practices, energy efficiency, and eco-friendly technologies reduce environmental impact.

k. Accessibility: Ensure that your physical location and digital assets are accessible to all, including individuals with disabilities, in compliance with accessibility standards.

l. Maintenance and Upkeep: Regular maintenance and upkeep of infrastructure are critical to prevent downtime and costly repairs.

5. Infrastructure Case Study: Amazon's Fulfillment Centers

Amazon, one of the world's largest e-commerce companies, has revolutionized the retail industry through its innovative infrastructure, particularly its fulfillment centers. These massive warehouses are strategically located across the globe and serve as the heart of Amazon's logistics operations. Here's how Amazon's infrastructure contributes to its success:

a. Strategic Placement: Amazon strategically places fulfillment centers in close proximity to major population centers. This minimizes shipping times and costs, enhancing the customer experience.

b. Advanced Automation: Fulfillment centers feature state-of-the-art automation technology, including robots that assist with order picking and packing. This increases efficiency and reduces labor costs.

c. Inventory Management: Amazon's sophisticated inventory management system ensures that products are readily available, reducing stockouts and optimizing storage space.

d. Shipping Optimization: The company's logistics infrastructure includes a vast fleet of delivery vehicles, drones, and partnerships with carriers to ensure timely and cost-effective shipping.

e. Data-Driven Decisions: Amazon leverages data analytics to make informed decisions about inventory, shipping routes, and customer preferences.

f. Scalability: Amazon's fulfillment centers are designed for scalability. During peak seasons like the holidays, the company can quickly ramp up operations to meet increased demand.

g. Robotics and Technology: Amazon continually invests in robotics and technology to enhance the efficiency of its fulfillment centers.

h. Customer-Centric Approach: By focusing on fast and reliable order fulfillment, Amazon maintains a strong reputation for customer satisfaction.

6. Leveraging Location and Infrastructure for Success

Now that we've explored the significance of location and infrastructure, it's crucial to understand how entrepreneurs can leverage these elements to their advantage. Just as skilled navigators harness the wind and tides, entrepreneurs can optimize their business environment for success:

a. Location-Based Marketing: Use your location as a marketing tool. Highlight your proximity to key amenities, landmarks, or industry hubs in your branding and communications.

b. Network Locally: Engage with local business associations, chambers of commerce, and networking events to build connections and partnerships within your community.

c. Talent Recruitment: Leverage your location to attract top talent. If you're situated in a tech hub, for example, emphasize the opportunities for tech professionals to join your team.

d. Infrastructure Investment: Continuously invest in your infrastructure to ensure it meets the evolving needs of your business. Modernize your digital systems, expand your physical space, and adopt eco-friendly technologies when feasible.

e. Regulatory Compliance: Stay informed about local regulations and compliance requirements. Develop a compliance strategy that ensures your operations adhere to all relevant laws.

f. Adaptability: Be open to adapting your location or infrastructure as your business evolves. If your market shifts, consider expanding or relocating to better align with customer demand.

g. Innovation: Use your infrastructure as a foundation for innovation. Explore how technology and automation can enhance your operations and customer experience.

h. Sustainability: Embrace sustainability as part of your infrastructure strategy. Implement eco-friendly practices and communicate your commitment to environmental responsibility.

i. Disaster Preparedness: Develop robust disaster recovery and contingency plans to safeguard your business in the event of unforeseen disruptions.

j. Scalability: Plan for scalability from the outset. Ensure that your infrastructure can accommodate growth without major disruptions to your operations.

k. Customer-Centric Approach: Prioritize customer convenience and satisfaction in your location and infrastructure decisions. Consider how your choices impact the customer experience.

l. Data-Driven Insights: Leverage data analytics to gain insights into customer behavior, market trends, and operational efficiency. Use this data to make informed decisions about your location and infrastructure.

7. Conclusion: Navigating Success Through Location and Infrastructure

In the intricate tapestry of entrepreneurship, location and infrastructure are the threads that weave together the story of business success.

 Just as skilled navigators choose their course wisely and maintain their vessels, entrepreneurs must carefully select their business location and invest in robust infrastructure.

The choice of location can determine your access to customers, talent, resources, and growth opportunities. A well-planned infrastructure ensures that your operations run smoothly, efficiently, and sustainably.

When these elements align with your business goals and strategy, they become powerful tools that propel your venture forward.

As you navigate the entrepreneurial waters, remember that the significance of location and infrastructure extends beyond bricks and mortar.

They are dynamic assets that can be leveraged to enhance your brand, customer relationships, and competitive advantage.

In your entrepreneurial journey, let location be the canvas upon which you paint your vision, and let infrastructure be the scaffolding that supports your dreams.

With careful consideration, strategic planning, and adaptability, you can harness the power of location and infrastructure to chart a course toward business success, leaving an indelible mark on the entrepreneurial landscape.

CHAPTER SIX
Human Resources and Team Building

In the intricate fabric of entrepreneurship, human resources (HR) and team building are the threads that weave together the tapestry of success. Much like a conductor harmonizes an orchestra, effective HR practices and cohesive team dynamics orchestrate the symphony of business operations, productivity, and growth.

This exploration delves into the essential role of HR and team building in entrepreneurship, unraveling the strategies that foster a motivated workforce, nurture leadership, and cultivate an environment conducive to achieving business objectives.

1. The Essence of Human Resources: Cultivating a Flourishing Workforce

Human resources is more than just a department; it's the driving force that nurtures, develops, and empowers the individuals who power your business.

HR encompasses a range of activities, from recruitment and training to performance management and employee engagement. At its core, effective HR aims to create a positive work environment that maximizes employee potential and aligns with business goals. Here are key aspects of HR in entrepreneurship:

a. Recruitment and Selection: Hiring the right individuals is the foundation of a strong team. Define clear job roles, skill requirements, and cultural fit to attract candidates who align with your vision.

b. Onboarding: Smooth onboarding sets the tone for an employee's experience. Provide comprehensive orientation, training, and resources to help new hires integrate quickly and effectively.

c. Training and Development: Continuous learning and skill development are essential for both individual and organizational growth. Offer training programs, workshops, and opportunities for employees to enhance their skills.

d. Performance Management: Regularly assess employee performance and provide feedback. Performance reviews help identify strengths, address weaknesses, and set goals.

e. Employee Engagement: Engaged employees are more productive and committed. Foster engagement through open communication, recognition programs, and opportunities for involvement.

f. Compensation and Benefits: Competitive compensation and attractive benefits packages are essential for attracting and retaining top talent.

g. Diversity and Inclusion: Embrace diversity and create an inclusive workplace where all employees feel valued, respected, and able to contribute their unique perspectives.

h. Employee Well-being: Prioritize the well-being of your employees by promoting work-life balance, mental health support, and a healthy workplace culture.

2. Building a High-Performing Team: The Art of Collaboration

A business is only as good as its employees. Building a high-performing team requires more than assembling a group of individuals; it entails fostering a collaborative environment where diverse skills, talents, and personalities converge to achieve shared goals. Here's how to create a cohesive and effective team:

a. Clear Roles and Responsibilities: Define roles, responsibilities, and expectations clearly to avoid confusion and overlapping tasks.

b. Communication: Open, transparent, and effective communication is the cornerstone of successful teamwork. Encourage regular communication, active listening, and feedback.

c. Trust and Respect: Nurture an environment of trust and respect where team members feel safe expressing ideas, challenging assumptions, and sharing feedback.

d. Shared Goals: Align team members around common objectives. When everyone understands the bigger picture, collaboration becomes more purposeful.

e. Skill Diversity: Assemble a team with diverse skills and strengths that complement each other. A well-rounded team can tackle challenges from multiple angles.

f. Empowerment: Empower team members to make decisions and take ownership of their work. Autonomy fosters motivation and accountability.

g. Conflict Resolution: Conflicts are inevitable, but addressing them constructively is essential. Implement processes for resolving conflicts and encourage open dialogue.

h. Recognition and Celebration: Recognize and celebrate team achievements and milestones. Acknowledging hard work boosts morale and reinforces a sense of accomplishment.

3. Leadership and Management: Navigating the Path of Guidance

In the entrepreneurial landscape, leadership plays a pivotal role in steering the ship toward success. Effective leadership goes beyond management; it inspires, motivates, and guides the team to achieve their best. Whether you're a sole proprietor or leading a larger team, here are key leadership principles to consider:

a. Lead by Example: Leadership is about setting the tone. Show your team the values, work ethic, and behavior you expect.

b. Communication Skills: Effective communication is a hallmark of strong leadership. Clearly convey expectations, provide feedback, and listen to your team.

c. Emotional Intelligence: Being attuned to your own emotions and those of others fosters empathy, understanding, and better decision-making.

d. Delegation: Trust your team by delegating tasks and responsibilities. Delegation empowers team members and frees you to focus on strategic priorities.

e. Vision and Strategy: Articulate a clear vision for the business and the path to achieve it. Leaders inspire when they communicate a compelling future.

f. Adaptability: The business landscape is dynamic. Leaders must adapt to changes, seize opportunities, and navigate challenges with resilience.

g. Mentorship and Development: Invest in the growth of your team members. Provide mentorship, opportunities for skill development, and guidance for career advancement.

h. Conflict Resolution: Address conflicts promptly and objectively. Effective conflict resolution maintains a positive team dynamic.

4. Motivation and Employee Engagement: Fostering a Culture of Purpose

A motivated and engaged workforce is the heartbeat of a successful business. Motivation goes beyond financial incentives; it's about creating an environment where employees are inspired to contribute their best efforts. Here's how to foster motivation and engagement:

a. Meaningful Work: Help employees see the impact of their work on the business and its customers. When employees understand the value they provide, their motivation increases.

b. Recognition and Rewards: Acknowledge and appreciate employee contributions through recognition programs, awards, and incentives.

c. Growth Opportunities: Provide avenues for professional and personal growth within the company. Employees are more engaged when they see a clear path for advancement.

d. Flexibility: Offer flexible work arrangements that accommodate employees' needs and promote work-life balance.

e. Regular Feedback: Provide consistent feedback, both positive and constructive. Feedback helps employees understand their strengths and areas for improvement.

f. Employee Voice: Encourage employees to share their opinions, ideas, and concerns. Listening to employee input shows that their opinions are appreciated.

g. Team Building Activities: Organize team-building activities that foster camaraderie, trust, and collaboration among team members.

5. Adapting to Remote Work and Hybrid Models: Navigating the New Normal

The global landscape of work has transformed, with remote work and hybrid models becoming increasingly common. Entrepreneurs must adapt their HR practices and team dynamics to these changing work environments. Here's how:

a. Remote Work Policies: Establish clear policies for remote work, outlining expectations, communication protocols, and performance measurement.

b. Technology and Infrastructure: Provide the necessary tools and technology to ensure remote team members can collaborate effectively.

c. Communication: Maintain open lines of communication with remote team members through video calls, messaging apps, and regular check-ins.

d. Flexibility: Embrace flexibility in work hours and arrangements to accommodate remote team members' different needs and time zones.

e. Team Bonding: Despite physical distance, prioritize team bonding activities to strengthen relationships and maintain a sense of belonging.

6. Handling Challenges and Resilience: Navigating Stormy Waters

Entrepreneurship is not without challenges. How you navigate adversity and lead your team through difficult times shapes the resilience and success of your business. Here's how to handle challenges and maintain a resilient team:

a. Transparent Communication: During challenging times, communicate openly with your team about the situation, plans, and potential solutions.

b. Problem-solving: Encourage a problem-solving mindset within your team. Collaboratively address challenges and explore innovative solutions.

c. Emotional Support: Show empathy and provide emotional support to team members facing challenges. A supportive environment fosters resilience.

d. Learning from Failure: Treat failures as opportunities for growth. Encourage your team to learn from mistakes and apply those lessons to future endeavors.

e. Adaptability: In rapidly changing circumstances, flexibility and adaptability are key. Be willing to pivot your strategies and make necessary adjustments.

Sailing Toward Success Together

Human resources and team building are the compass and crew that guide your entrepreneurial ship through the waters of success.

By cultivating a thriving workforce, building a cohesive team, demonstrating effective leadership, nurturing motivation and engagement, adapting to evolving work models, and handling challenges with resilience, you create an environment in which people work together to achieve common goals.

Just as skilled navigation ensures a ship reaches its destination, adept HR practices and strong team dynamics ensure your business sails toward sustainable success, no matter the challenges or opportunities that arise along the way.

CHAPTER SEVEN
Product/Service Development

In the dynamic landscape of entrepreneurship, product and service development is the compass that guides businesses toward innovation, market relevance, and sustainable growth. Just as explorers embark on journeys of discovery with maps and tools, entrepreneurs navigate the complexities of creating new offerings by combining creativity, market insights, and strategic planning.

This exploration delves into the intricacies of product and service development, unveiling the strategies that fuel innovation, meet customer needs, and pave the way for business success.

1. The Essence of Product/Service Development: Creating Value

Product and service development is not solely about bringing new offerings to the market; it's about creating value for customers. Whether you're launching a physical product or an intangible service, the development process revolves around identifying and addressing customer needs, pain points, and desires.

It's a meticulous journey that involves ideation, research, design, testing, and iteration. Here's a closer look at the key components of product and service development:

a. Idea Generation: Ideas are the seeds of innovation. Encourage brainstorming sessions, research trends, and engage with customer feedback to generate innovative concepts.

b. Market Research: Thorough market research is the foundation of successful development. Understand your target audience, competitors, and market trends to inform your product/service strategy.

c. Concept Development: Refine your ideas into viable concepts that align with customer needs and market demand. Consider features, benefits, pricing, and positioning.

d. Design and Prototyping: Design is where ideas come to life. Create prototypes or mock-ups to visualize your product/service and gather feedback for improvements.

e. Testing and Validation: Test your prototype with a select group of customers to gather insights and identify potential flaws or areas for enhancement.

f. Iteration: Based on feedback and testing results, iterate on your design and features to create a more refined version that better addresses customer needs.

g. Production/Implementation: Once your product/service is ready, initiate production or implementation processes, ensuring quality control and consistency.

h. Launch and Marketing: Develop a comprehensive marketing strategy to introduce your offering to the market. Highlight its unique value and benefits to attract customers.

i. Continuous Improvement: The journey doesn't end with launch. Continuously gather feedback, monitor performance, and make improvements based on customer input and market trends.

2. Customer-Centric Approach: Meeting Market Needs

A successful product or service is one that meets a genuine market need. Entrepreneurs must be attuned to customer preferences, pain points, and behaviors to develop offerings that resonate. Here's how to adopt a customer-centric approach to product/service development:

a. Empathy and Understanding: Put yourself in the shoes of your customers. Understand their challenges, aspirations, and motivations to tailor your offerings accordingly.

b. Voice of the Customer: Gather direct input from customers through surveys, focus groups, interviews, and online feedback. This firsthand insight informs your development decisions.

c. Problem-Solving: Your offering should solve a specific problem or address a pain point for your target audience. Identify these pain points and design solutions that directly alleviate them.

d. User Experience (UX) Design: Prioritize user-friendliness and a seamless experience. A well-designed and user-friendly interface improves consumer happiness.

e. Persona Development: Create customer personas that represent different segments of your target audience. This helps you tailor your development efforts to specific needs and preferences.

f. Co-Creation: Involve customers in the development process. Seek their feedback at various stages to ensure your offering aligns with their expectations.

3. Innovation and Differentiation: Standing Out in the Crowd

In a competitive marketplace, innovation is the key to differentiation. Your product or service needs to stand out from the crowd and offer something unique that captures customer attention. Here's how to infuse innovation into your product/service development process:

a. Market Gap Analysis: Identify gaps in the market where there is a lack of offerings that address specific needs. Develop solutions that fill these gaps.

b. Creativity and Ideation: Encourage a culture of creativity within your team. Set aside time for brainstorming and idea-sharing sessions to foster innovative thinking.

c. Unique Selling Proposition (USP): Define your offering's USP—the unique value it provides that sets it apart from competitors. Communicate this USP clearly in your marketing.

d. Technology Integration: Explore how emerging technologies can enhance your offering. Incorporating cutting-edge technology can provide a competitive edge.

e. Sustainability: Consider environmental and ethical factors in your product/service development. Sustainability and social responsibility can be powerful points of differentiation.

f. Continuous Learning: Stay informed about industry trends, technological advancements, and changing consumer behaviors. Continuous learning fuels your ability to innovate.

4. Market Validation: Ensuring Demand and Viability

Before investing significant resources into product/service development, it's crucial to validate the demand and viability of your offering in the market. Market validation involves gathering evidence that customers are willing to pay for your solution. Here's how to ensure demand and viability:

a. Minimum Viable Product (MVP): Develop a stripped-down version of your offering with essential features. Test this MVP in the market to gauge interest and collect feedback.

b. Pre-Sales and Pre-Orders: Offer pre-sales or pre-order options to gauge customer interest before full-scale production or launch.

c. Crowdfunding: Platforms like Kickstarter and Indiegogo allow you to test the market and secure funding before fully developing your product.

d. Surveys and Focus Groups: Conduct surveys and focus groups to assess customer reactions and preferences before committing to the full development process.

e. Pilot Launch: Launch your offering in a limited market or region to gather real-world data on its performance and customer acceptance.

5. Agile Development: Flexibility and Iteration

Agile development is an approach that emphasizes flexibility, collaboration, and iterative progress. It's particularly useful in dynamic markets where customer needs and preferences evolve rapidly. Here's how to adopt agile principles in your product/service development process:

a. Cross-Functional Teams: Form multidisciplinary teams that bring together diverse expertise, from design to engineering to marketing.

b. Iterative Design: Develop your offering in stages, gathering feedback and making improvements after each iteration.

c. Regular Feedback Loops: Maintain open lines of communication with customers and stakeholders throughout the development process. Incorporate their feedback to refine your offering.

d. Rapid Prototyping: Create prototypes quickly to visualize concepts and gather feedback before investing in full development.

e. Test and Learn: Implement features or changes on a smaller scale to assess their impact before rolling them out to a broader audience.

6. Intellectual Property Protection: Safeguarding Your Innovations

Innovative products and services often come with valuable intellectual property (IP) that needs protection. Whether it's a unique design, a novel technology, or a proprietary process, safeguarding your IP is essential to maintaining your competitive advantage. Here's how to protect your innovations:

a. Patents: Consider applying for patents to protect new inventions or processes. Patents grant exclusive rights to use, make, and sell the patented invention.

b. Trademarks: Register trademarks for distinctive names, logos, and symbols associated with your offering. Trademarks prevent others from using similar marks that could cause confusion.

c. Copyrights: If your offering involves creative content, such as software, designs, or written materials, consider securing copyrights to protect your original works.

d. Trade Secrets: Keep sensitive information, such as proprietary formulas or manufacturing processes, confidential as trade secrets.

e. Non-Disclosure Agreements (NDAs): Use NDAs when sharing confidential information with partners, suppliers, or collaborators to prevent unauthorized disclosure.

7. Scaling and Continuous Improvement: Evolving with Success

After successfully launching your product or service, the journey doesn't end. Scaling and continuous improvement are essential to keep your offering relevant and responsive to changing market dynamics. Here's how to ensure your product/service evolves with success:

a. Scalability: Ensure that your production, distribution, and customer support processes can handle increased demand as your business grows.

b. Feedback Integration: Continue gathering customer feedback and insights to identify areas for improvement and inform updates.

c. Feature Updates: Regularly introduce new features or enhancements to your offering based on customer needs and technological advancements.

d. Customer Support: Provide robust customer support to address inquiries, issues, and feedback. Positive customer experiences contribute to loyalty and referrals.

e. Monitoring and Analysis: Continuously monitor metrics, such as sales data, customer satisfaction, and usage patterns, to identify trends and make data-driven decisions.

Sailing Toward Innovation and Market Success

Product and service development is the vessel that carries entrepreneurs on a journey of innovation, customer satisfaction, and business success.

By adopting a customer-centric approach, embracing innovation, validating market demand, fostering agility, protecting intellectual property, and focusing on scaling and improvement, you equip yourself to navigate the complexities of development and emerge with offerings that resonate in the marketplace.

Just as skilled navigators sail toward new horizons, entrepreneurs sail toward innovation and market success by creating offerings that inspire, solve problems, and exceed customer expectations.

CHAPTER EIGHT
Branding and Marketing

In the vast ocean of business, branding, and markcting serve as the sails and compass that guide companies toward their destination of customer connection, market relevance, and sustainable growth. Just as skilled navigators use the stars to chart their course, entrepreneurs rely on strategic branding and marketing to navigate the competitive landscape and build strong relationships with their target audiences.

This exploration delves into the multifaceted realm of branding and marketing, uncovering the strategies that underpin effective communication, brand identity, customer engagement, and long-term business success.

1. The Essence of Branding and Marketing: The Heartbeat of Connection

Branding and marketing are not just promotional tools; they are the heartbeat of your business's identity and connection with customers. Branding shapes the perception of your business in the minds of consumers, while marketing is the vehicle through which you communicate your brand's value and offerings.

Together, they create a powerful narrative that resonates with customers and distinguishes your business in the marketplace. Here's a closer look at the key components of branding and marketing:

a. Brand Identity: Develop a clear and consistent brand identity that encompasses your business's values, mission, personality, and visual elements. This identity becomes the foundation of your brand's story.

b. Messaging: Craft compelling and authentic messaging that communicates your brand's value proposition, resonates with your target audience and addresses their needs.

c. Visual Identity: Design a cohesive visual identity that includes logos, color palettes, typography, and imagery. Consistency across all visual elements reinforces brand recognition.

d. Marketing Channels: Identify the most relevant and effective marketing channels to reach your target audience. This could include digital platforms, social media, traditional advertising, events, and more.

e. Content Creation: Develop high-quality content that educates, entertains, or solves problems for your audience. Valuable content establishes your brand as an authority in your industry.

f. Customer Engagement: Foster meaningful interactions with your audience through engagement strategies, such as responding to comments, hosting contests, and initiating conversations.

g. Data Analysis: Leverage data and analytics to track the effectiveness of your branding and marketing efforts. Use insights to refine your strategies and make data-driven decisions.

h. Storytelling: Craft a compelling brand story that resonates emotionally with your audience. Authentic storytelling humanizes your brand and forges deeper connections.

2. Brand Strategy: Setting the Course for Connection

A well-defined brand strategy is the compass that guides your branding efforts toward creating a lasting and meaningful connection with customers. It's the intentional plan that ensures every aspect of your brand, from visuals to messaging, is aligned and consistent. Here's how to develop a robust brand strategy:

a. Target Audience: Clearly define your target audience by considering demographics, psychographics, behaviors, and preferences. Tailor your branding to resonate with this specific group.

b. Brand Positioning: Determine where your brand stands in relation to competitors. Highlight your unique value proposition and the aspects that set your brand apart.

c. Brand Voice and Personality: Define your brand's voice—how you communicate—and its personality—how you're perceived. Is your brand playful, serious, empathetic, or authoritative?

d. Core Values: Identify the core values that your brand embodies. These values guide decision-making, shape your culture, and resonate with like-minded customers.

e. Visual Identity: Develop a visual identity that aligns with your brand's personality and resonates with your target audience. Consistency in all graphic components strengthens brand awareness.

f. Brand Guidelines: Create brand guidelines that outline how your brand should be represented across different touchpoints, ensuring consistency in tone, visuals, and messaging.

g. Emotional Connection: Craft a brand narrative that evokes emotions and connects with your audience on a deeper level. Storytelling makes your brand memorable and relatable.

h. Brand Loyalty: Build a loyal customer base by consistently delivering on your brand promise. Satisfied customers become brand advocates and contribute to positive word-of-mouth.

3. Integrated Marketing: Navigating Multichannel Engagement

Integrated marketing is the art of delivering a cohesive and seamless experience to your audience across various marketing channels. It ensures that your brand message remains consistent and impactful regardless of where customers interact with it. Here's how to execute an effective integrated marketing strategy:

a. Channel Selection: Choose the marketing channels that align with your target audience's preferences and behaviors. This could include social media, email marketing, content marketing, events, and more.

b. Consistent Messaging: Craft messaging that remains consistent across all channels. Your brand's tone, value proposition, and key messages should resonate uniformly.

c. Visual Cohesiveness: Maintain a consistent visual identity across all channels. Visual cohesion reinforces brand recognition and professionalism.

d. Omnichannel Experience: Ensure a seamless transition as customers move between different channels. An omnichannel experience enhances customer satisfaction and engagement.

e. Cross-Promotion: Cross-promote content and offerings across different channels to reinforce messages and increase visibility.

f. Data Integration: Integrate data from various channels to gain a holistic view of customer behavior and preferences. This data-driven approach informs future marketing decisions.

g. Customer Journeys: Map out customer journeys across different touchpoints, from initial awareness to post-purchase engagement. Tailor content and messaging to each stage of the journey.

h. Performance Measurement: Use analytics to measure the performance of each channel and assess their contribution to overall marketing objectives. Allocate resources based on data-driven insights.

4. Digital Branding and Online Presence: Navigating the Digital Landscape

In today's digital age, a strong online presence is essential for effective branding and marketing. Digital branding encompasses how your brand is perceived in the digital space, from websites to social media platforms. Here's how to navigate the digital landscape:

a. User-Centric Website: Design a user-friendly website that provides a seamless experience for visitors. Your website often serves as the initial point of contact for prospective customers.

b. Search Engine Optimization (SEO): Optimize your website and content for search engines to increase visibility in search results and attract organic traffic.

c. Social Media Strategy: Develop a comprehensive social media strategy that aligns with your brand's voice and values. Engage with followers, share valuable content, and build relationships.

d. Content Marketing: Create valuable and relevant content that addresses your audience's needs. Blog posts, videos, infographics, and eBooks establish your brand as an industry authority.

e. Email Marketing: Build and nurture an email list to stay connected with your audience. Email marketing is an effective way to share updates, promotions, and valuable content.

f. Online Advertising: Use online advertising platforms, such as Google Ads and social media ads, to reach your target audience with targeted messages.

g. Influencer Partnerships: Collaborate with influencers or thought leaders in your industry to extend your brand's reach and credibility.

h. Online Reputation Management: Monitor and manage your brand's online reputation by responding to reviews, comments, and feedback.

5. Customer Engagement and Relationship Building: Nurturing Connections

Effective branding and marketing go beyond one-time transactions; they focus on building long-lasting relationships with customers. Customer engagement involves creating meaningful interactions and experiences that foster loyalty and advocacy. Here's how to cultivate customer engagement and relationship building:

a. Personalization: Tailor your communication and offerings to individual customer preferences. Personalization enhances the customer experience and demonstrates that you understand their needs.

b. Social Listening: Monitor social media and online platforms to understand customer sentiment, address concerns, and engage in conversations about your brand.

c. Two-Way Communication: Foster open and genuine two-way communication with customers. Respond to queries, suggestions, and comments as soon as possible.

d. Loyalty Programs: Create loyalty programs that reward repeat customers. These programs incentivize customers to continue engaging with your brand.

e. Customer Feedback: Encourage customers to provide feedback and actively listen to their suggestions. Feedback can guide improvements and demonstrate your commitment to their satisfaction.

f. Customer Support: Provide exceptional customer support that resolves issues promptly and professionally. Positive support experiences contribute to customer loyalty.

g. Social Engagement: Engage with customers on social media by responding to comments, sharing user-generated content, and hosting interactive campaigns.

h. Community Building: Create a sense of community around your brand. Host webinars, workshops, or events that bring like-minded customers together.

6. Brand Evolution and Adaptation: Navigating Change

Branding is not static; it evolves and adapts to reflect changes in your business, industry, and customer preferences. To remain relevant and resonant, your brand must be open to transformation while retaining its core identity. Here's how to navigate brand evolution and adaptation:

a. Market Research: Continuously conduct market research to understand shifting customer needs, industry trends, and competitive landscape.

b. Rebranding: Consider rebranding if your current brand identity no longer aligns with your goals or resonates with your target audience.

c. Brand Extensions: Introduce new products or services that complement your existing offerings and align with your brand's values.

d. Cultural Relevance: Stay attuned to cultural shifts and societal changes. Ensure that your brand remains inclusive and relevant to diverse audiences.

e. Consistency Amid Change: While adapting, maintain consistency in core brand elements to avoid confusion among existing customers.

f. Storytelling of Transformation: Communicate your brand's evolution transparently and authentically to customers. Share the journey of change through storytelling.

g. Employee Alignment: Ensure that employees understand and embrace the evolving brand narrative. Internal alignment enhances the external projection of the brand.

h. Customer Involvement: Involve customers in the evolution process. Seek their input and feedback to create a brand that resonates with their preferences.

7. Crisis Management and Brand Resilience: Navigating Stormy Waters

In the face of challenges, a strong brand is a beacon of trust and resilience. Effective crisis management preserves your brand's integrity and safeguards customer loyalty. Here's how to navigate crisis management and build brand resilience:

a. Preparedness: Develop a comprehensive crisis management plan that outlines roles, responsibilities, and communication strategies for different scenarios.

b. Transparent Communication: During crises, communicate openly and honestly with customers. Provide updates, address concerns, and share steps being taken to resolve the situation.

c. Swift Action: Take swift and decisive action to address the crisis and minimize its impact. Putting customer safety and satisfaction first demonstrates your commitment to their well-being.

d. Social Media Management: Monitor social media closely during crises and respond promptly to customer inquiries and comments.

e. Rebuilding Trust: After a crisis, work on rebuilding customer trust. Implement preventative efforts to avoid such events in future periods.

f. Consistency and Authenticity: Maintain brand consistency and authenticity even in times of crisis. Your response should align with your brand's values and messaging.

g. Learning and Improvement: After the crisis subsides, conduct a thorough review to identify lessons learned and areas for improvement in crisis management.

h. Customer Support: Provide exceptional customer support during and after a crisis. Your response can shape perceptions of your brand's resilience and commitment to customer welfare.

Sailing Toward Connection and Business Triumph

Branding and marketing are the guiding stars that illuminate the path to customer connection and business triumph.

By crafting a compelling brand identity, mapping a strategic marketing course, embracing digital opportunities, fostering customer engagement, adapting to change, and mastering crisis management, you equip your business to navigate the dynamic waters of entrepreneurship with confidence.

Just as skilled navigators set sail toward distant shores, entrepreneurs set sail toward meaningful customer connections, market relevance, and long-lasting success by building brands that inspire, engage, and endure.

CHAPTER NINE
Customer Acquisition

In the intricate realm of entrepreneurship, customer acquisition stands as the compass that guides businesses toward growth, profitability, and long-term success. Much like skilled navigators who chart their course through uncharted waters, entrepreneurs must navigate the complexities of attracting, converting, and retaining customers in a dynamic and competitive landscape. This exploration delves into the multifaceted world of customer acquisition, uncovering the strategies that underpin effective lead generation, conversion optimization, and building lasting customer relationships.

1. The Essence of Customer Acquisition: The Fuel for Business Growth

Customer acquisition is not just a transactional process; it's the lifeblood of business growth. It encompasses the strategies, tactics, and methodologies that businesses employ to capture the attention of potential customers, convert them into paying clients, and forge relationships that foster loyalty and repeat business. At its core, customer acquisition is about creating a seamless and compelling journey that guides prospects from awareness to engagement and, ultimately, to becoming valued customers. Here's a closer look at the key components of effective customer acquisition:

a. Lead Generation: Identify and attract potential customers who express interest in your products or services. Effective lead generation fuels the pipeline of potential clients.

b. Conversion Optimization: Fine-tune the process of turning leads into customers. Conversion optimization involves enhancing user experiences, addressing objections, and reducing friction points.

c. Relationship Building: Forge meaningful and lasting relationships with customers through excellent service, personalized interactions, and ongoing engagement.

d. Retention Strategies: Implement strategies to retain existing customers, as they provide a valuable source of recurring revenue and referrals.

e. Data-Driven Insights: Utilize data and analytics to understand customer behavior, preferences, and pain points. Data-driven insights inform your customer acquisition strategies.

f. Omni-channel Approach: Engage with potential customers across multiple channels, both online and offline, to maximize reach and exposure.

g. Tailored Communication: Craft tailored and relevant communication that addresses the unique needs and challenges of different customer segments.

2. Lead Generation: Casting the Net for Prospects

Lead generation is the cornerstone of customer acquisition—it's the process of attracting and capturing potential customers' interest in your products or services. Effective lead-generation strategies provide a steady stream of prospects who are likely to be interested in what your business offers. Here's how to navigate the waters of lead generation:

a. Target Audience Definition: Clearly define your target audience based on demographics, behaviors, interests, and pain points. Understand who your ideal customers are.

b. Content Marketing: Develop valuable and informative content that addresses your audience's challenges and questions. Content marketing promotes and ranks your company as an industry authority.

c. Search Engine Optimization (SEO): Optimize your online presence to ensure that your website and content are discoverable by potential customers searching for relevant keywords.

d. Social Media Engagement: Utilize social media platforms to engage with your target audience, share content, and build a community around your brand.

e. Email Marketing: Build and nurture an email list by offering valuable content, promotions, and insights in exchange for contact information.

f. Webinars and Workshops: Host webinars, workshops, or online events that provide educational value to potential customers and showcase your expertise.

g. Landing Pages: Create dedicated landing pages that highlight specific offers, benefits, or solutions. Landing pages are designed to capture contact information from interested visitors.

h. Lead Magnets: Offer lead magnets, such as eBooks, whitepapers, or templates, as incentives for prospects to provide their contact information.

i. Referral Programs: Encourage existing customers to refer potential leads to your business in exchange for rewards or discounts.

3. Conversion Optimization: Guiding Leads to Become Customers

Conversion optimization is the art of guiding leads through the journey of becoming paying customers. This involves minimizing friction, addressing objections, and creating a seamless process that encourages prospects to take the desired action. Here's how to optimize your conversion process:

a. User-Friendly Website: Ensure that your website is intuitive, user-friendly, and optimized for various devices. A positive browsing experience increases the likelihood of conversions.

b. Compelling Call-to-Action (CTA): Use clear and compelling CTAs that prompt visitors to take action. CTAs should be strategically placed on relevant pages.

c. Landing Page Optimization: Optimize landing pages for specific offers or products. Maintain consistency between the ad or link that brings users to the landing page and the content they find there.

d. A/B Testing: Conduct A/B testing to compare different versions of your pages, CTAs, and messaging to determine which elements drive higher conversion rates.

e. Clear Value Proposition: Communicate the unique value and benefits that your products or services offer. Explain how they address specific pain points or fulfill needs.

f. Trust Signals: Include trust signals such as customer reviews, testimonials, industry certifications, and security badges to instill confidence in your prospects.

g. Friction Reduction: Simplify the conversion process by minimizing the number of steps required and avoiding unnecessary form fields.

h. Exit Intent Pop-ups: Use exit-intent pop-ups to capture contact information from visitors who are about to leave your site.

i. Social Proof: Showcase evidence of your brand's popularity, such as the number of customers served or positive media coverage.

4. Relationship Building: Fostering Customer Loyalty

Building strong relationships with customers is a cornerstone of successful customer acquisition. It involves going beyond the initial transaction to create a positive and memorable experience that leads to loyalty, repeat business, and referrals. Here's how to foster lasting relationships:

a. Personalized Communication: Tailor your communication to individual customers based on their preferences, purchase history, and interactions with your brand.

b. Exceptional Customer Service: Provide excellent customer support that exceeds expectations. Responsive and helpful customer service builds trust.

c. Loyalty Programs: Implement loyalty programs that reward repeat customers with exclusive offers, discounts, or rewards.

d. Follow-Up and Engagement: Follow up with customers after a purchase to ensure satisfaction, gather feedback, and address any concerns.

e. Customer Feedback: Actively seek and value customer feedback. Feedback helps you understand customer perceptions and make improvements.

f. Social Media Engagement: Engage with customers on social media platforms, responding to comments, acknowledging mentions, and participating in discussions.

g. Personalized Offers: Offer personalized promotions or discounts based on customer preferences and purchase history.

h. Surveys and Feedback: Conduct surveys to understand customer needs, preferences, and pain points. Use insights to refine your offerings and customer experience.

i. Community Building: Create a sense of community around your brand by hosting events, forums, or online groups where customers can connect and share experiences.

5. Customer Retention Strategies: Navigating the Waters of Loyalty

Keeping current clients is just as crucial as gaining new ones. Repeat business not only contributes to revenue but also serves as a testament to your brand's quality and customer satisfaction. Here's how to navigate the waters of customer retention:

a. Customer Education: Provide resources and guides that help customers maximize the value of your products or services.

b. Exclusive Content: Offer exclusive content, such as advanced tutorials, tips, or industry insights, to loyal customers.

c. Subscription Models: If applicable, offer subscription-based models that provide ongoing value and convenience to customers.

d. Personalized Recommendations: Use customer data to provide personalized product recommendations that align with their interests and needs.

e. Email Marketing: Regularly communicate with your existing customers through email campaigns that offer value, updates, and promotions.

f. Feedback Incorporation: Act on customer feedback by making improvements to your products, services, or customer experience.

g. Anniversary Offers: Celebrate customer milestones, such as anniversaries of their first purchase, with special offers or discounts.

h. Customer Recognition: Acknowledge and celebrate loyal customers publicly through social media shout-outs or customer spotlights.

i. Proactive Problem Solving: Anticipate potential issues and address them proactively to ensure customer satisfaction.

6. Data-Driven Insights: Navigating with Precision

Data-driven insights play a crucial role in customer acquisition by providing a deep understanding of customer behavior, preferences, and pain points. These insights empower businesses to refine their strategies and tailor their approach to different customer segments. Here's how to leverage data-driven insights for effective customer acquisition:

a. Analytics Tools: Utilize analytics tools to gather data on website traffic, user behavior, conversion rates, and other key metrics.

b. Customer Segmentation: Segment your audience based on demographics, behaviors, purchase history, and preferences.

c. A/B Testing: Conduct A/B testing to compare different approaches and determine which strategies yield the best results.

d. Customer Journey Mapping: Map out the customer journey from the initial touchpoint to conversion and beyond. Identify pain points and opportunities for improvement.

e. Purchase Funnel Analysis: Analyze the stages of the purchase funnel to identify where potential customers drop off or lose interest.

f. Heatmaps and Session Recordings: Use heatmaps and session recordings to understand how users navigate your website and interact with different elements.

g. Social Listening: Monitor social media platforms and online discussions to gain insights into customer sentiment and trends.

h. Email Campaign Analytics: Analyze email campaign performance to understand open rates, click-through rates, and engagement levels.

i. Conversion Rate Optimization (CRO): Continuously optimize your website and landing pages based on CRO best practices and data-driven insights.

7. Omni-channel Approach: Navigating Multifaceted Engagement

In today's interconnected world, an omni-channel approach to customer acquisition is essential. An omni-channel strategy ensures consistent and cohesive engagement with potential customers across various touchpoints, whether online or offline. Here's how to navigate an omni-channel approach:

a. Channel Integration: Integrate different marketing channels to provide a seamless experience for customers as they transition between channels.

b. Consistent Messaging: Maintain consistent messaging and branding across all channels to reinforce your brand's identity.

c. Mobile Optimization: Ensure that your online presence, including your website and emails, is optimized for mobile devices.

d. Social Media Integration: Integrate social media platforms into your customer acquisition strategy to engage with potential customers and share valuable content.

e. Email and SMS Campaigns: Combine email marketing with SMS campaigns to reach customers through multiple communication channels.

f. In-Person Engagement: If applicable, incorporate in-person events, workshops, or pop-up stores to connect with customers face-to-face.

g. Customer Service: Provide consistent and excellent customer service across all channels, including phone, email, chat, and social media.

h. Personalization: Tailor your communication and offerings to the channel and platform being used by the customer.

i. Data Syncing: Ensure that customer data is synchronized across different systems and platforms to provide a unified view of customer interactions.

8. Tailored Communication: Navigating Personalized Engagement

Personalized communication is a cornerstone of effective customer acquisition. It involves tailoring your messaging, offers, and interactions to the specific preferences and needs of individual customers. Here's how to navigate personalized engagement:

a. Customer Segmentation: Divide your audience into segments based on common characteristics, behaviors, and preferences.

b. Dynamic Content: Use dynamic content to display different messaging or offers based on the user's profile or behavior.

c. Behavioral Triggers: Set up automated triggers that send relevant messages or offers based on specific customer actions.

d. Personalized Recommendations: Offer product or service recommendations based on the customer's purchase history and browsing behavior.

e. Abandoned Cart Recovery: Send personalized emails to customers who abandoned their shopping carts, reminding them of their unfinished purchase.

f. Personalized Subject Lines: Customize email subject lines to increase open rates and engagement.

g. Geo-Targeting: Tailor offers and promotions based on the customer's location or local events.

h. Retargeting Campaigns: Use retargeting ads to display relevant products or services to customers who have previously visited your website.

i. Preference Centers: Allow customers to set their communication preferences, ensuring that they receive content that aligns with their interests.

9. Influencer and Partner Collaborations: Navigating Collaborative Acquisition

Collaborating with influencers, industry experts, and partners can significantly enhance your customer acquisition efforts. These collaborations leverage the trust and credibility that influencers and partners have already established with their audiences. Here's how to navigate collaborative acquisition:

a. Identify Relevant Influencers: Choose influencers or partners whose audience aligns with your target demographic and values.

b. Genuine Partnerships: Build genuine relationships with influencers and partners. Emphasize upon mutual benefits and common aims.

c. Co-Created Content: Collaborate with influencers to create content that resonates with their audience and showcases your products or services.

d. Affiliate Marketing: Set up affiliate programs where partners earn commissions for driving leads or sales to your business.

e. Guest Blogging: Contribute guest posts to industry websites and blogs to reach new audiences and establish your brand as an authority.

f. Webinars and Joint Events: Host webinars, workshops, or events in partnership with influencers or experts in your industry.

g. Social Media Takeovers: Allow influencers to take over your social media accounts for a day to engage with their audience using your brand's voice.

h. Influencer Reviews: Encourage influencers to review your products or services and share their experiences with their followers.

i. Cross-Promotion: Cross-promote each other's content, products, or services to expand reach and engagement.

10. Continuous Optimization: Navigating the Path of Improvement

Customer acquisition is an ongoing journey that requires continuous optimization and adaptation. Businesses must be agile and willing to refine their strategies based on customer feedback, market trends, and data-driven insights. Here's how to navigate the path of continuous optimization:

a. Regular Analysis: Continuously analyze the performance of your customer acquisition efforts through data metrics, conversion rates, and ROI.

b. Feedback Incorporation: Incorporate customer feedback to refine your approach and address pain points.

c. Testing and Experimentation: Regularly test new strategies, channels, and messaging to identify what resonates best with your target audience.

d. Benchmarking: Benchmark your customer acquisition performance against industry standards and competitors to identify areas for improvement.

e. Evolving Technologies: Stay updated with emerging technologies and tools that can enhance your customer acquisition efforts.

f. Adaptation to Trends: Stay attuned to changing customer behaviors, market trends, and technological advancements that may impact your strategy.

g. Training and Skill Development: Invest in training and skill development for your team to ensure they are equipped to execute effective customer acquisition strategies.

h. Customer-Centric Approach: Keep the customer at the center of your strategies, making sure your approach aligns with their needs and preferences.

i. Celebrate Successes: Celebrate milestones and successes in customer acquisition to motivate your team and reinforce the importance of their efforts.

Sailing Toward Growth and Prosperity

Customer acquisition is the compass that guides businesses toward growth, prosperity, and enduring success. By mastering lead generation, optimizing conversion processes, fostering customer relationships, retaining loyalty, leveraging data-driven insights, embracing an omnichannel approach, personalizing communication, collaborating with influencers, and embracing continuous improvement, entrepreneurs navigate the complex waters of customer acquisition with confidence. Just as skilled navigators navigate the seas with precision and finesse, businesses sail toward growth and prosperity by acquiring and nurturing customers who believe in their brand, products, and services.

CHAPTER TEN
Sales and Distribution

In the intricate landscape of business, the processes of sales and distribution form the compass that guides companies toward market penetration, revenue generation, and sustainable profitability.

Similar to skilled navigators who chart their course through uncharted waters, entrepreneurs must navigate the complex realm of sales and distribution to effectively reach customers, convert leads into buyers, and ensure that products and services are efficiently delivered. This exploration delves into the multifaceted world of sales and distribution, uncovering the strategies that underpin effective sales techniques, distribution networks, channel partnerships, and customer satisfaction.

1. The Essence of Sales and Distribution: Engines of Revenue

Sales and distribution are more than mere transactional activities; they are the engines that power a business's revenue generation and market expansion. Sales encompass the process of identifying potential buyers, guiding them through the purchasing journey, and ultimately converting them into paying customers. Distribution, on the other hand, focuses on the efficient movement of products and services from the manufacturer to the end consumer. Together, these processes constitute the lifeline of a business, ensuring that its offerings are accessible, valuable, and available to the target market. Here's a closer look at the key components of effective sales and distribution:

a. Sales Techniques: Mastering the art of sales involves employing a range of techniques to engage, educate, and persuade potential buyers.

b. Distribution Networks: Establishing distribution networks and channels that effectively reach target customers while minimizing logistics challenges.

c. Channel Partnerships: Collaborating with partners, resellers, and intermediaries to expand reach and leverage their expertise.

d. Customer Satisfaction: Ensuring a seamless buying experience, from order placement to product delivery, to foster repeat business and positive referrals.

e. Inventory Management: Efficiently managing inventory levels to balance supply and demand, avoiding overstock or stockouts.

f. Pricing Strategy: Develop a pricing strategy that aligns with the value proposition of the product or service and the target market's willingness to pay.

g. Sales Analytics: Utilizing data and analytics to measure sales performance, identify trends, and make informed strategic decisions.

h. After-Sales Support: Providing post-purchase support, warranties, and customer service to enhance customer satisfaction.

i. Geographic Reach: Expanding the business's reach into new geographic markets, whether local, regional, national, or international.

2. Sales Techniques: Navigating the Art of Persuasion

Sales techniques are the strategic maneuvers and interpersonal skills that sales professionals employ to guide potential customers toward making a purchase decision. Effective sales techniques involve understanding customer needs, building rapport, addressing objections, and presenting a compelling value proposition. Here's how to navigate the art of persuasion in sales:

a. Customer-Centric Approach: Place the customer's needs and preferences at the center of your sales strategy. Tailor your approach to their unique challenges.

b. Active Listening: Listen actively to understand the customer's pain points, preferences, and goals. Effective listening builds trust and rapport.

c. Consultative Selling: Position yourself as a consultant who offers valuable insights and solutions tailored to the customer's needs.

d. Value Proposition: Clearly articulate the unique value and benefits that your product or service provides. Explain how it addresses specific pain points.

e. Storytelling: Use storytelling to illustrate how your product or service has positively impacted other customers. Stories resonate emotionally and enhance credibility.

f. Handling Objections: Anticipate and address objections that customers may raise, providing factual and relevant responses to alleviate concerns.

g. Upselling and Cross-Selling: Identify opportunities to upsell customers on higher-value offerings or cross-sell complementary products or services.

h. Building Trust: Establish trust by demonstrating expertise, providing transparent information, and fulfilling promises.

i. Social Proof: Showcase customer testimonials, case studies, and success stories to provide evidence of the value your offerings deliver.

3. Distribution Networks: Navigating Reach and Efficiency

Distribution networks encompass the infrastructure, processes, and partners that facilitate the movement of products and services from manufacturers to end consumers. An efficient distribution network ensures that products are available when and where customers need them, optimizing accessibility and customer satisfaction. Here's how to navigate the complexities of distribution networks:

a. Market Research: Conduct thorough market research to understand the distribution preferences and behaviors of your target audience.

b. Channel Selection: Choose distribution channels that align with your target market's preferences and buying habits. Options include direct sales, retailers, wholesalers, e-commerce, and more.

c. Logistics Management: Establish efficient logistics processes to manage inventory, transportation, warehousing, and order fulfillment.

d. Supply Chain Collaboration: Collaborate with suppliers, manufacturers, and intermediaries to ensure a seamless flow of products through the supply chain.

e. Regional Considerations: Tailor your distribution approach to specific regions or markets, considering cultural preferences, regulatory requirements, and infrastructure.

f. E-commerce Integration: If applicable, integrate e-commerce platforms and online marketplaces to expand reach and accessibility.

g. Real-Time Tracking: Implement tracking and monitoring systems to provide real-time visibility into the status and location of products in transit.

h. Last-Mile Delivery: Optimize last-mile delivery to ensure timely and reliable product delivery to the end consumer.

i. Returns and Reverse Logistics: Develop a strategy for handling product returns and managing the reverse logistics process.

4. Channel Partnerships: Navigating Collaboration for Growth

Channel partnerships involve collaborating with resellers, distributors, retailers, and intermediaries to extend the reach of your products or services. These partnerships leverage the expertise and market presence of channel partners to tap into new customer segments and geographic markets. Here's how to navigate effective channel partnerships:

a. Partner Selection: Choose partners that align with your brand values, target market, and distribution goals. Evaluate their credibility and reputation.

b. Mutual Benefits: Establish partnerships that provide mutual benefits for both parties. Clearly define expectations and terms of the partnership.

c. Training and Support: Provide training and support to channel partners to ensure they have a deep understanding of your offerings and can effectively represent them.

d. Co-Marketing: Collaborate on marketing efforts with channel partners to jointly promote products or services.

e. Loyalty Programs: Implement loyalty programs that incentivize channel partners to actively promote and sell your offerings.

f. Clear Communication: Maintain open and transparent communication with channel partners to address challenges, share insights, and align strategies.

g. Performance Measurement: Monitor the performance of channel partners and assess their contribution to sales goals and objectives.

h. Exclusive Partnerships: Consider exclusive partnerships with key channel partners in specific markets to establish a strong presence.

i. Feedback Loop: Establish a feedback loop with channel partners to gather insights about customer preferences, challenges, and emerging trends.

5. Customer Satisfaction: Navigating the Road to Loyalty

Customers who are satisfied are more likely to become recurrent buyers, offer favorable referrals, and contribute to the growth of your company. Ensuring a smooth and delightful buying experience is essential for building customer loyalty. Here's how to navigate the road to customer satisfaction:

a. Seamless Ordering Process: Simplify the ordering process, whether through online platforms, in-person sales, or other channels.

b. Order Accuracy: Ensure that orders are processed accurately and that customers receive the products or services they expect.

c. Timely Delivery: Meet or exceed delivery expectations by providing timely and reliable product delivery.

d. Customer Communication: Keep customers informed about order status, shipping updates, and any potential delays.

e. Transparent Pricing: Provide clear and transparent pricing information to prevent surprises and build trust.

f. After-Sales Support: Offer post-purchase support, warranty information, and easy access to customer service for inquiries or concerns.

g. Return and Refund Policy: Establish a clear and customer-friendly return and refund policy to address any dissatisfaction or issues.

h. Feedback Collection: Actively seek customer feedback to understand their experiences, preferences, and suggestions for improvement.

i. Personalization: Tailor the customer experience to individual preferences whenever possible, enhancing the sense of value and care.

6. Inventory Management: Navigating Balance and Efficiency

Inventory management is the art of maintaining optimal stock levels to meet customer demand while avoiding overstocking or stockouts. Effective inventory management requires a delicate balance between supply and demand to ensure that products are available when customers need them. Here's how to navigate the challenges of inventory management:

a. Demand Forecasting: Utilize historical sales data, market trends, and customer insights to forecast demand accurately.

b. Safety Stock: Maintain a safety stock buffer to account for unexpected fluctuations in demand or supply chain disruptions.

c. Just-in-Time (JIT): Implement JIT inventory management to reduce holding costs and improve efficiency.

d. ABC Analysis: Classify inventory items based on their value and significance, focusing on managing high-value items more closely.

e. Inventory Tracking: Implement inventory tracking systems to monitor stock levels, reorder points, and lead times.

f. Supplier Relationships: Cultivate strong relationships with suppliers to ensure timely deliveries and favorable terms.

g. Seasonal Adjustments: Adjust inventory levels to accommodate seasonal demand fluctuations and trends.

h. Technology Integration: Utilize inventory management software and technologies to streamline processes and enhance accuracy.

i. Performance Metrics: Monitor key inventory performance metrics, such as turnover rate, carrying costs, and stockouts.

7. Pricing Strategy: Navigating Value and Profitability

Pricing strategy is a delicate balance between providing value to customers and ensuring the business's profitability. Effective pricing requires consideration of factors such as production costs, competitive landscape, perceived value, and the target market's willingness to pay. Here's how to navigate the intricacies of pricing strategy:

a. Cost-Based Pricing: Set prices based on production costs, including materials, labor, overhead, and desired profit margins.

b. Value-Based Pricing: Determine prices based on the perceived value that your product or service offers to customers.

c. Competitive Pricing: Analyze the pricing strategies of competitors to position your offerings competitively in the market.

d. Dynamic Pricing: Implement dynamic pricing models that adjust prices based on factors such as demand, time of purchase, and customer segment.

e. Bundle Pricing: Offer product bundles or packages that provide cost savings and value to customers.

f. Psychological Pricing: Utilize pricing strategies that leverage psychological triggers, such as ending prices with 9 or 99.

g. Premium Pricing: Position your offerings as premium products or services and set prices accordingly to reflect their exclusivity or unique features.

h. Price Testing: Conduct price testing and experiments to determine the optimal price point that maximizes revenue.

i. Price Transparency: Provide clear and transparent pricing information to build trust and avoid customer dissatisfaction.

8. Sales Analytics: Navigating Insights for Growth

Sales analytics involves the utilization of data and insights to measure sales performance, identify trends, and make informed strategic decisions. Data-driven insights empower businesses to refine their sales strategies, optimize processes, and allocate resources effectively. Here's how to navigate the path of sales analytics:

a. Data Collection: Gather relevant sales data, including revenue, conversion rates, customer demographics, and transaction details.

b. Data Integration: Integrate sales data with other business data, such as marketing analytics, customer feedback, and inventory levels.

c. Key Performance Indicators (KPIs): Identify and track key sales KPIs, such as customer acquisition cost, average order value, and sales growth.

d. Sales Funnel Analysis: Analyze the stages of the sales funnel to identify drop-offs and areas for improvement.

e. Customer Segmentation: Segment customers based on behavior, demographics, purchase history, and preferences.

f. Sales Forecasting: Utilize historical data and trends to forecast future sales, helping in resource allocation and planning.

g. Competitive Analysis: Analyze competitors' sales data and strategies to identify opportunities and threats.

h. Data Visualization: Use data visualization tools to present insights in a clear and understandable format.

i. Continuous Improvement: Continuously analyze sales data to identify opportunities for optimization and enhancement.

9. After-Sales Support: Navigating the Path of Customer Care

After-sales support is a critical component of customer satisfaction and retention. It involves providing ongoing assistance, support, and service to customers after they have made a purchase. Effective after-sales support enhances the overall customer experience and contributes to repeat business and positive referrals. Here's how to navigate the path of after-sales support:

a. Help Center and FAQs: Provide a comprehensive help center or FAQs section that addresses common questions and concerns.

b. Customer Service: Offer multiple channels for customers to reach out for support, including phone, email, live chat, and social media.

c. Technical Assistance: Provide technical assistance for products or services that require installation, setup, or troubleshooting.

d. Warranty and Return Policy: Clearly communicate warranty terms and return policies to customers to avoid confusion.

e. Proactive Communication: Reach out to customers after their purchase to ensure satisfaction, gather feedback, and offer assistance.

f. Knowledge Base: Develop a knowledge base that offers detailed information and guides for using your products or services.

g. Continuous Training: Train customer support representatives to provide accurate and effective assistance.

h. Personalized Support: Tailor support interactions to individual customer needs and preferences.

i. Feedback Incorporation: Use customer feedback from support interactions to identify areas for improvement and enhance the overall customer experience.

10. Geographic Reach: Navigating New Markets and Borders

Expanding geographic reach involves entering new markets and regions to tap into additional customer segments and opportunities. Navigating the complexities of global expansion requires consideration of cultural differences, regulatory requirements, and market trends. Here's how to navigate the challenges of geographic reach:

a. Market Research: Conduct thorough market research to understand the cultural, economic, and demographic characteristics of the target market.

b. Localization: Adapt your offerings, messaging, and communication to align with the cultural preferences and language of the new market.

c. Regulatory Compliance: Ensure that your products and services comply with local regulations and standards.

d. Distribution Channels: Establish or adapt distribution channels that are effective in the new market.

e. Competitive Analysis: Understand the competitive landscape in the new market and identify opportunities for differentiation.

f. Marketing Strategies: Develop marketing strategies that resonate with the preferences and behaviors of the new target audience.

g. Logistics and Supply Chain: Establish efficient logistics and supply chain processes to ensure timely product delivery.

h. Partnerships and Alliances: Consider partnerships or alliances with local businesses or organizations to navigate cultural nuances and build credibility.

i. Pilot Programs: Launch pilot programs to test the waters and gather insights before scaling up operations in the new market.

Sailing Toward Market Penetration and Profitability

Sales and distribution are the navigational tools that guide businesses toward market penetration, revenue growth, and sustainable profitability. By mastering sales techniques, establishing efficient distribution networks, fostering channel partnerships, prioritizing customer satisfaction, optimizing inventory management, refining pricing strategies, leveraging sales analytics, providing after-sales support, expanding geographic reach, and embracing continuous improvement, entrepreneurs navigate the complex waters of sales and distribution with finesse. Just as skilled navigators steer their vessels through uncharted territories with precision, businesses sail toward market dominance and financial success by effectively reaching customers, delivering value, and ensuring a seamless buying experience.

CHAPTER ELEVEN
Adaptation and Learning

In the dynamic landscape of business, the ability to adapt and learn stands as the compass that guides organizations through uncertainty, change, and innovation.

Just as skilled navigators adjust their course to navigate changing tides and weather conditions, successful businesses must continually adapt to shifting market trends, technological advancements, and customer preferences.

This exploration delves into the multifaceted world of adaptation and learning, uncovering the strategies that underpin resilience, agility, innovation, and continuous improvement.

1. The Essence of Adaptation and Learning: Thriving Amidst Change

Adaptation and learning are not just reactive survival mechanisms; they are proactive strategies that empower businesses to thrive in a rapidly changing environment. Adaptation involves adjusting strategies, processes, and operations to align with emerging challenges and opportunities.

Learning, on the other hand, encompasses acquiring new knowledge, skills, and insights that drive innovation and growth. Together, adaptation and learning enable businesses to remain relevant, competitive, and responsive to customer needs. Here's a closer look at the key components of effective adaptation and learning:

a. Resilience: Building the capacity to withstand disruptions, setbacks, and unexpected events without losing momentum.

b. Agility: Developing the ability to quickly pivot, change direction, and seize new opportunities as they arise.

c. Innovation: Embracing creativity and experimentation to develop new products, services, processes, and business models.

d. Continuous Improvement: Cultivating a culture of ongoing evaluation and refinement to enhance efficiency, quality, and customer satisfaction.

e. Market Insight: Staying attuned to market trends, customer preferences, and competitive forces to inform strategic decisions.

f. Technological Awareness: Keeping up-to-date with technological advancements that could impact your industry and business operations.

g. Customer-Centric Approach: Focusing on understanding and meeting the evolving needs and expectations of your target audience.

h. Risk Management: Identifying and mitigating potential risks and challenges before they escalate.

i. Adaptive Leadership: Cultivating leaders who are open to change, lead by example, and encourage a culture of adaptation and learning.

2. Resilience: Navigating Unpredictability with Grace

Resilience is the foundation of adaptation—it's the ability to bounce back from challenges, setbacks, and unexpected disruptions. Just as skilled navigators navigate stormy waters with poise, businesses must navigate uncertainty with grace and resilience. Here's how to foster resilience in the face of adversity:

a. Scenario Planning: Anticipate potential challenges and develop contingency plans to address various scenarios.

b. Crisis Management: Establish protocols for managing crises, including communication plans and response strategies.

c. Flexibility: Build flexibility into your business processes, allowing for adjustments when unexpected events occur.

d. Team Empowerment: Empower your team to make decisions and take initiative during times of uncertainty.

e. Learning from Failure: Embrace failures as learning opportunities, extracting insights that inform future strategies.

f. Mental Health Support: Provide resources and support to help employees cope with stress and challenges.

g. Diverse Perspectives: Encourage diverse perspectives and ideas to foster innovative solutions to challenges.

h. Customer Communication: Maintain open and transparent communication with customers during disruptions to build trust.

i. Resource Allocation: Allocate resources strategically to support critical functions and initiatives during challenging times.

3. Agility: Navigating Change with Speed and Precision

Agility is the art of responding swiftly and decisively to change. Like skilled navigators adjusting their sails to changing winds, agile businesses pivot their strategies and operations to capitalize on emerging opportunities. Here's how to navigate the path of agility:

a. Cross-Functional Collaboration: Foster collaboration across departments to enable rapid decision-making and execution.

b. Data-Driven Insights: Utilize data and analytics to make informed, real-time decisions that align with market dynamics.

c. Iterative Processes: Embrace iterative processes that allow for frequent adjustments based on feedback and changing conditions.

d. Scalable Infrastructure: Build scalable systems and infrastructure that can accommodate growth and sudden changes in demand.

e. Rapid Prototyping: Use rapid prototyping and testing to quickly validate new ideas and concepts before full-scale implementation.

f. Customer-Centric Iteration: Continuously iterate based on customer feedback and evolving preferences.

g. Delegation of Authority: Delegate decision-making authority to appropriate levels of the organization to expedite execution.

h. Scenario Simulation: Conduct scenario simulations to prepare for potential changes and their impacts on the business.

i. Digital Transformation: Embrace digital tools and technologies that enhance operational efficiency and responsiveness.

4. Innovation: Navigating New Horizons of Creativity

Innovation is the compass that guides businesses toward new horizons of creativity, discovery, and growth. Like skilled navigators charting unexplored waters, innovative businesses seek uncharted opportunities and develop novel solutions to address evolving needs. Here's how to navigate the realm of innovation:

a. Idea Generation: Encourage employees at all levels to contribute ideas and solutions for innovation.

b. Design Thinking: Implement design thinking principles to understand customer needs and develop user-centric solutions.

c. Cross-Industry Inspiration: Draw inspiration from other industries and fields to spark fresh ideas and approaches.

d. Prototyping and Testing: Rapidly prototype and test new ideas to gauge feasibility and user response.

e. Innovation Labs: Create dedicated spaces or teams focused on experimenting with new concepts and technologies.

f. Open Innovation: Collaborate with external partners, startups, and research institutions to co-create innovative solutions.

g. Continuous Learning: Encourage a culture of continuous learning, where employees are empowered to explore new skills and knowledge.

h. Risk-Taking: Foster a culture that encourages calculated risk-taking and experimentation.

i. Innovation Metrics: Define metrics to measure the success and impact of innovation initiatives.

5. Continuous Improvement: Navigating the Path of Excellence

Continuous improvement is the journey toward excellence that businesses undertake. Like skilled navigators refining their routes for optimal efficiency, businesses embrace a culture of refinement and enhancement to achieve operational excellence. Here's how to navigate the path of continuous improvement:

a. Kaizen Philosophy: Adopt the Kaizen philosophy of incremental improvement as a foundational principle.

b. Process Mapping: Map out existing processes to identify inefficiencies, bottlenecks, and areas for improvement.

c. Employee Involvement: Involve employees in the improvement process, as they often have valuable insights from the front lines.

d. Data-Driven Analysis: Utilize data and analytics to identify patterns, trends, and areas for optimization.

e. Lean Principles: Implement lean principles to eliminate waste, reduce unnecessary steps, and streamline processes.

f. Benchmarking: Compare your processes and performance against industry best practices and competitors.

g. Continuous Training: Provide ongoing training and skill development to ensure that employees are equipped to drive improvement.

h. Employee Recognition: Recognize and reward employees who contribute innovative ideas and suggestions for improvement.

i. Feedback Loop: Establish a feedback loop with customers and stakeholders to gather insights for refinement.

6. Market Insight: Navigating Customer Preferences and Trends

Market insight is the compass that guides businesses toward understanding customer preferences, behaviors, and emerging trends.

Like skilled navigators studying ocean currents and weather patterns, businesses must gather and analyze data to make informed decisions about products, services, and strategies. Here's how to navigate the realm of market insight:

a. Customer Surveys: Conduct regular surveys to gather feedback on customer satisfaction, preferences, and pain points.

b. Data Analytics: Utilize data analytics tools to track customer behavior, purchasing patterns, and engagement metrics.

c. Social Listening: Monitor social media platforms and online discussions to gain insights into customer sentiment and trends.

d. Competitor Analysis: Study your competitors to identify their strengths, weaknesses, and areas of differentiation.

e. Trend Forecasting: Stay attuned to emerging industry trends, technological advancements, and cultural shifts.

f. Focus Groups: Organize focus groups to gather qualitative insights directly from your target audience.

g. Customer Persona Development: Create detailed customer personas that represent different segments of your target market.

h. Data Privacy: Ensure that customer data is collected and used in compliance with relevant data privacy regulations.

i. Continuous Feedback: Maintain an ongoing dialogue with customers to understand their evolving needs and expectations.

7. Technological Awareness: Navigating the Digital Landscape

Technological awareness is the compass that guides businesses through the ever-evolving digital landscape. Like skilled navigators keeping track of navigation instruments, businesses must stay informed about technological advancements that can impact their industry, operations, and customer engagement. Here's how to navigate the realm of technological awareness:

a. Continuous Learning: Foster a culture of continuous learning and professional development to keep employees up-to-date with technology trends.

b. Technology Partnerships: Collaborate with technology partners, startups, and experts to stay informed about emerging solutions.

c. Industry Conferences: Attend industry conferences, webinars, and workshops to stay updated on technological advancements.

d. Innovation Labs: Establish innovation labs or research units dedicated to exploring and experimenting with new technologies.

e. Pilot Projects: Implement pilot projects to test the feasibility and impact of new technologies before full-scale adoption.

f. Cloud Computing: Embrace cloud computing to enhance scalability, accessibility, and data storage.

g. Automation: Explore automation solutions to streamline repetitive tasks and improve efficiency.

h. Data Security: Prioritize data security and compliance with relevant regulations to protect customer and business information.

i. User Experience: Use technology to enhance user experiences across digital platforms, applications, and interactions.

8. Customer-Centric Approach: Navigating Evolving Needs and Expectations

A customer-centric approach is the compass that guides businesses toward understanding and meeting the evolving needs and expectations of their customers.

Like skilled navigators aligning their course with the desires of their passengers, businesses must prioritize customer satisfaction, engagement, and loyalty. Here's how to navigate the realm of customer-centricity:

a. Customer Journey Mapping: Map out the customer journey to understand touchpoints, pain points, and opportunities for improvement.

b. Personalization: Tailor marketing messages, product recommendations, and experiences to individual customer preferences.

c. Feedback Collection: Regularly gather feedback from customers to understand their experiences and identify areas for enhancement.

d. Customer Support: Provide exceptional customer support through multiple channels, addressing inquiries and concerns promptly.

e. Loyalty Programs: Implement loyalty programs that reward repeat customers and encourage ongoing engagement.

f. Empathy Training: Train employees to empathize with customer needs and emotions, creating a positive interaction.

g. Data Privacy: Handle customer data with care and respect for their privacy preferences and legal regulations.

h. Voice of the Customer: Incorporate the "voice of the customer" into decision-making processes to prioritize their preferences.

i. Relationship Building: Build long-term relationships with customers by maintaining communication and providing value beyond transactions.

9. Risk Management: Navigating Uncertainty with Preparedness

Risk management is the compass that guides businesses in navigating uncertainties and potential threats. Like skilled navigators assessing navigational hazards, businesses must identify, assess, and mitigate risks that could impact their operations, reputation, and growth. Here's how to navigate the realm of risk management:

a. Risk Assessment: Regularly assess potential risks and their potential impact on your business operations.

b. Risk Mitigation Strategies: Develop strategies to mitigate identified risks, whether through prevention, transfer, or contingency planning.

c. Business Continuity Planning: Create plans for business continuity in the event of disruptions, emergencies, or unforeseen events.

d. Compliance: Stay informed about industry regulations, laws, and standards to ensure legal and ethical practices.

e. Cybersecurity: Implement robust cybersecurity measures to protect against data breaches and cyber threats.

f. Crisis Communication: Develop a crisis communication plan to manage communication during times of adversity.

g. Insurance Coverage: Consider insurance coverage options that provide protection against specific risks.

h. Supplier Risk Management: Assess and manage risks associated with suppliers, ensuring a stable supply chain.

i. Employee Training: Educate employees about risk management practices and their role in mitigating potential threats.

10. Adaptive Leadership: Navigating Change from the Helm

Adaptive leadership is the compass that guides organizations through change from the helm. Like skilled navigators leading their crew through shifting waters, adaptive leaders inspire, guide, and empower their teams to embrace change and drive innovation.

Here's how to navigate the realm of adaptive leadership:

a. Vision Communication: Clearly communicate a compelling vision for change and the benefits it will bring to the organization.

b. Emotional Intelligence: Cultivate emotional intelligence to understand and address the concerns and motivations of your team.

c. Empowerment: Empower employees to take ownership of their roles, make decisions, and contribute to change initiatives.

d. Flexibility: Demonstrate flexibility and adaptability in response to feedback, new information, and unexpected challenges.

e. Conflict Resolution: Address conflicts and disagreements constructively, promoting a culture of open dialogue and resolution.

f. Coaching and Mentorship: Provide coaching and mentorship to support employees in adapting to new roles or responsibilities.

g. Leading by Example: Model the behavior and mindset you expect from your team when navigating change.

h. Continuous Learning: Lead by example in embracing continuous learning and personal growth.

i. Celebrate Progress: Celebrate milestones and achievements on the journey of change to boost morale and motivation.

Sailing Toward Innovation and Longevity

Adaptation and learning are the twin compasses that guide businesses toward innovation, resilience, and longevity. By fostering resilience, embracing agility, driving innovation, pursuing continuous improvement, seeking market insight, staying technologically aware, prioritizing the customer, managing risks, practicing adaptive leadership, and nurturing a culture of learning, entrepreneurs navigate the complex waters of business with confidence.

Just as skilled navigators weather storms, chart new courses, and explore uncharted territories, businesses sail toward innovation and long-term success by adapting to change, seizing opportunities, and continually enhancing their capabilities.

CHAPTER TWELVE
Financial Management

In the intricate landscape of business, financial management serves as the compass that guides organizations toward fiscal responsibility, sustainability, and growth. Like skilled navigators charting their course through complex waters, entrepreneurs must navigate the realm of financial management to effectively allocate resources, manage cash flow, make informed investment decisions, and ensure the long-term financial health of their businesses. This exploration delves into the multifaceted world of financial management, uncovering the strategies that underpin sound fiscal strategy, risk mitigation, capital allocation, and profitability.

1. The Essence of Financial Management: Building a Strong Financial Foundation

Financial management is not merely about balancing books and recording transactions; it's about building a strong financial foundation that supports the strategic goals and growth aspirations of a business. Effective financial management involves planning, organizing, controlling, and monitoring financial resources to optimize their utilization and achieve desired outcomes. Here's a closer look at the key components of effective financial management:

a. Budgeting and Forecasting: Developing budgets and forecasts that guide spending, revenue projections, and resource allocation.

b. Cash Flow Management: Monitoring and managing cash inflows and outflows to ensure liquidity and meet financial obligations.

c. Investment Analysis: Analyzing investment opportunities to allocate capital to projects that provide the highest return on investment.

d. Risk Management: Identifying, assessing, and mitigating financial risks that could impact the stability and growth of the business.

e. Financial Reporting: Generating accurate and timely financial reports that provide insights into the company's financial health and performance.

f. Cost Control: Implementing strategies to control costs, minimize wastage, and optimize operational efficiency.

g. Debt Management: Managing debt obligations and ensuring that the business's borrowing aligns with its financial capabilities.

h. Financial Governance: Establishing policies, controls, and procedures to ensure compliance with financial regulations and standards.

i. Capital Structure: Determining the optimal mix of equity and debt financing to fund the business's operations and growth.

2. Budgeting and Forecasting: Navigating Financial Planning

Budgeting and forecasting are the navigational tools that guide businesses through the process of financial planning. Like skilled navigators plotting their course, businesses develop budgets and forecasts to allocate resources effectively, plan for growth, and anticipate financial challenges. Here's how to navigate the path of budgeting and forecasting:

a. Revenue Projections: Estimate future revenues based on historical performance, market trends, and growth strategies.

b. Expense Estimation: Forecast anticipated expenses, including fixed costs, variable costs, and one-time expenditures.

c. Capital Expenditures: Plan for major capital expenditures, such as equipment purchases or facility expansions.

d. Sensitivity Analysis: Perform sensitivity analysis to understand how changes in key variables impact the budget and financial performance.

e. Rolling Forecasts: Adopt a rolling forecast approach that continually updates projections based on real-time data and market changes.

f. Scenario Planning: Develop multiple budget scenarios based on different assumptions to prepare for varying outcomes.

g. Budget Review: Regularly review and adjust the budget to ensure alignment with business goals and market conditions.

h. Performance Tracking: Monitor actual financial performance against the budget and analyze variances.

i. Flexibility: Build flexibility into the budget to accommodate unexpected changes and opportunities.

3. Cash Flow Management: Navigating Liquidity and Financial Stability

Cash flow management is the compass that guides businesses in navigating the waters of liquidity and financial stability. Like skilled navigators assessing their available supplies, businesses must manage cash inflows and outflows to ensure they have the resources needed to meet financial obligations and seize growth opportunities. Here's how to navigate the path of cash flow management:

a. Cash Flow Projection: Develop cash flow projections that forecast cash inflows and outflows on a regular basis.

b. Working Capital Management: Efficiently manage working capital components, such as accounts receivable, accounts payable, and inventory.

c. Credit Management: Implement effective credit policies to ensure timely collection of receivables and minimize bad debts.

d. Expense Control: Control discretionary spending to maintain a healthy cash balance and avoid unnecessary expenditures.

e. Emergency Reserves: Establish emergency reserves to cushion the business against unforeseen financial challenges.

f. Supplier Negotiations: Negotiate favorable terms with suppliers to optimize cash outflows.

g. Short-Term Financing: Consider short-term financing options, such as lines of credit or business loans, to cover temporary cash shortages.

h. Cash Flow Analysis: Conduct regular cash flow analysis to identify trends, patterns, and opportunities for improvement.

i. Investment of Excess Cash: Invest excess cash in short-term instruments to earn a return while maintaining liquidity.

4. Investment Analysis: Navigating Growth and ROI

Investment analysis is the compass that guides businesses in navigating growth opportunities and maximizing returns on investment. Like skilled navigators evaluating potential destinations, businesses must assess investment options to allocate capital to projects that align with their strategic objectives and deliver favorable returns. Here's how to navigate the path of investment analysis:

a. Risk-Return Assessment: Evaluate potential investments based on the balance between risk and potential return.

b. ROI Calculation: Calculate the return on investment (ROI) to determine the profitability of a project or initiative.

c. Payback Period: Determine the payback period—the time it takes for an investment to generate enough returns to cover its initial cost.

d. Net Present Value (NPV): Use NPV analysis to assess the value of future cash flows in today's terms, accounting for the time value of money.

e. Internal Rate of Return (IRR): Calculate the IRR to determine the rate at which an investment breaks even and generates positive returns.

f. Opportunity Cost: Consider the opportunity cost of investing in one project over another, factoring in potential benefits foregone.

g. Feasibility Study: Conduct feasibility studies to evaluate the viability and potential challenges of a proposed investment.

h. Sensitivity Analysis: Perform sensitivity analysis to understand how changes in key assumptions impact the investment's outcomes.

i. Diversification: Diversify investment portfolios to spread risk across different asset classes and reduce overall risk.

5. Risk Management: Navigating Financial Uncertainties

Risk management is the compass that guides businesses in navigating financial uncertainties and potential threats. Like skilled navigators anticipating navigational hazards, businesses must identify, assess, and mitigate financial risks that could impact their profitability, reputation, and growth prospects. Here's how to navigate the path of risk management:

a. Risk Identification: Identify potential financial risks, including market risks, credit risks, operational risks, and regulatory risks.

b. Risk Assessment: Assess the likelihood and potential impact of each identified risk on the business's financial performance.

c. Risk Mitigation Strategies: Develop strategies to mitigate identified risks, such as implementing internal controls, diversifying investments, or hedging.

d. Contingency Planning: Create contingency plans that outline how the business will respond if specific risks materialize.

e. Insurance Coverage: Consider insurance coverage options that provide protection against specific financial risks.

f. Compliance: Stay informed about financial regulations and standards to ensure compliance and avoid financial penalties.

g. Stress Testing: Conduct stress tests to evaluate how the business would perform under adverse economic conditions.

h. Risk Monitoring: Continuously monitor financial risks and adjust mitigation strategies as needed.

i. Risk Culture: Foster a risk-aware culture where employees are educated about potential risks and encouraged to report concerns.

6. Financial Reporting: Navigating Transparency and Accountability

Financial reporting is the compass that guides businesses in navigating transparency, accountability, and compliance with financial regulations. Like skilled navigators maintaining precise records, businesses must generate accurate and timely financial reports that provide insights into their financial performance and health. Here's how to navigate the path of financial reporting:

a. Accrual Accounting: Use accrual accounting to recognize revenues and expenses when they are earned or incurred, regardless of cash flow.

b. Financial Statements: Prepare key financial statements, including the balance sheet, income statement, and cash flow statement.

c. GAAP Compliance: Ensure compliance with Generally Accepted Accounting Principles (GAAP) or applicable financial reporting standards.

d. Audit Readiness: Keep accurate records and documentation to facilitate external audits, if required.

e. Transparency: Provide clear and transparent financial information to stakeholders, investors, and regulators.

f. Management Discussion and Analysis (MD&A): Include an MD&A section in financial reports to provide context and analysis of financial performance.

g. Key Performance Indicators (KPIs): Include relevant financial and non-financial KPIs in reports to assess business performance.

h. Timeliness: Generate financial reports in a timely manner to support decision-making and accountability.

i. Data Accuracy: Ensure the accuracy and reliability of financial data through regular reconciliations and validation processes.

7. Cost Control: Navigating Efficiency and Profitability

Cost control is the compass that guides businesses in navigating efficiency and profitability. Like skilled navigators conserving resources, businesses must implement strategies to control costs, minimize wastage, and optimize operational efficiency. Here's how to navigate the path of cost control:

a. Cost Analysis: Conduct detailed cost analysis to understand the breakdown of expenses across different functions and activities.

b. Cost Reduction Strategies: Develop strategies to reduce costs while maintaining quality and customer satisfaction.

c. Lean Principles: Implement lean principles to eliminate waste, unnecessary steps, and inefficiencies in processes.

d. Vendor Negotiations: Negotiate with vendors and suppliers to secure favorable terms, discounts, and bulk purchasing deals.

e. Technology Utilization: Use technology to automate processes, reduce manual tasks, and improve operational efficiency.

f. Energy Efficiency: Implement energy-efficient practices and technologies to reduce utility costs.

g. Outsourcing: Consider outsourcing non-core functions to reduce overhead and operating costs.

h. Employee Training: Train employees to be cost-conscious and empower them to contribute cost-saving ideas.

i. Benchmarking: Compare your costs and expenses to industry benchmarks and best practices to identify areas for improvement.

8. Debt Management: Navigating Financial Leverage

Debt management is the compass that guides businesses in navigating financial leverage and optimizing their capital structure. Like skilled navigators managing their ship's ballast, businesses must carefully consider the amount and type of debt to use in their financing mix to support growth and manage risk. Here's how to navigate the path of debt management:

a. Debt Capacity: Determine the business's ability to service debt obligations based on cash flow and financial health.

b. Debt-Equity Ratio: Assess the optimal debt-equity ratio that balances financial risk and flexibility.

c. Interest Rate Analysis: Evaluate interest rates and terms of potential debt financing options to minimize interest costs.

d. Repayment Planning: Develop repayment plans that align with the business's cash flow and growth trajectory.

e. Creditworthiness: Maintain a strong credit rating by fulfilling debt obligations and demonstrating financial stability.

f. Debt Covenants: Understand and comply with debt covenants to avoid defaults and maintain lender trust.

g. Refinancing: Evaluate opportunities to refinance existing debt to secure more favorable terms.

h. Short-Term vs. Long-Term Debt: Determine the appropriate balance between short-term and long-term debt based on the business's needs and financial goals.

i. Debt Restructuring: Consider debt restructuring options if the business faces financial challenges that impact its ability to meet debt obligations.

9. Financial Governance: Navigating Compliance and Accountability

Financial governance is the compass that guides businesses in navigating compliance with financial regulations and standards. Like skilled navigators adhering to maritime laws, businesses must establish and enforce policies, controls, and procedures to ensure ethical conduct, accurate reporting, and accountability. Here's how to navigate the path of financial governance:

a. Internal Controls: Implement internal controls that safeguard assets, prevent fraud, and ensure accurate financial reporting.

b. Segregation of Duties: Separate responsibilities within financial processes to minimize the risk of errors or fraud.

c. Audit Trails: Maintain detailed records and audit trails that provide transparency into financial transactions.

d. Code of Ethics: Establish a code of ethics that guides employees in making ethical financial decisions.

e. Compliance Framework: Develop a compliance framework that aligns with financial regulations and industry standards.

f. **Whistleblower Policies:** Implement whistleblower policies that allow employees to report financial misconduct confidentially.

g. Board Oversight: Provide board oversight and governance to ensure financial decisions align with the organization's strategic objectives.

h. Training and Education: Provide training and education to employees about financial governance principles and practices.

i. Continuous Improvement: Continuously review and enhance financial governance practices to adapt to changing regulations and business needs.

10. Capital Structure: Navigating Financing Strategies

Capital structure is the compass that guides businesses in navigating financing strategies to fund their operations and growth. Like skilled navigators adjusting their vessel's weight distribution, businesses must determine the optimal mix of equity and debt financing to maintain financial flexibility and minimize costs. Here's how to navigate the path of capital structure:

a. Equity Financing: Consider raising capital through equity financing, such as issuing shares to investors.

b. Debt Financing: Evaluate debt financing options, including bank loans, bonds, and lines of credit, to fund capital needs.

c. Hybrid Financing: Explore hybrid financing options that combine elements of both equity and debt financing.

d. Cost of Capital: Calculate the cost of capital associated with different financing sources to make informed decisions.

e. Financial Ratios: Monitor key financial ratios, such as debt-to-equity ratio and interest coverage ratio, to assess financial health.

f. Investor Relations: Maintain open communication with investors and shareholders about the business's financial performance and strategy.

g. Seasonal Financing: Plan for seasonal fluctuations in capital needs and ensure adequate funding during peak periods.

h. Retained Earnings: Consider using retained earnings as a source of internal financing for growth initiatives.

i. Dividend Policies: Determine dividend policies that balance returning value to shareholders with reinvesting in the business.

Sailing Toward Financial Prosperity

Financial management serves as the guiding compass that directs businesses toward fiscal prosperity, stability, and growth.

By mastering budgeting and forecasting, optimizing cash flow, analyzing investments, managing risks, ensuring accurate financial reporting, controlling costs, balancing debt, practicing sound financial governance, structuring capital wisely, and aligning financial strategies with business objectives, entrepreneurs navigate the intricate waters of financial management with precision.

Just as skilled navigators steer their vessels through changing tides and unforeseen challenges, businesses sail toward financial prosperity by making informed decisions, adapting to market dynamics, and maintaining a steadfast commitment to sound fiscal strategy.

CHAPTER THIRTEEN
Growth and Scaling

In the vast ocean of entrepreneurship, growth, and scaling serve as the compass that guides businesses toward expanded horizons, increased market presence, and enhanced profitability.

Just as skilled navigators chart their course through uncharted waters, entrepreneurs must navigate the dynamic landscape of growth, making strategic decisions, seizing opportunities, and overcoming challenges to steer their businesses toward success.

This exploration delves into the multifaceted world of growth and scaling, uncovering the strategies that underpin sustainable expansion, innovation, and long-term resilience.

1. Understanding Growth and Scaling: The Evolution of Entrepreneurship

Growth and scaling are not mere buzzwords; they represent the evolution of a business from its initial stages to a more established and thriving entity. While growth typically refers to an increase in size, revenue, or market share, scaling involves expanding the business's capacity to handle growth without proportional increases in resources. Here's a closer look at the key components of growth and scaling:

a. Organic vs. Strategic Growth: Organic growth involves expanding through increased sales and customer acquisition, while strategic growth involves deliberate initiatives such as mergers, acquisitions, or partnerships.

b. Horizontal vs. Vertical Scaling: Horizontal scaling involves expanding within the same market or industry, while vertical scaling entails expanding into different stages of the value chain.

c. Balanced Growth: Achieving a balanced growth trajectory that maintains a harmonious relationship between revenue, profitability, and operational capacity.

d. Innovation and Adaptation: Incorporating innovation and adaptability to navigate changing market dynamics and customer preferences.

e. Investment and Resources: Securing the necessary investment and resources to fuel growth initiatives effectively.

f. Scalability: Ensuring that the business's infrastructure, processes, and systems can handle increased demands and operational complexities.

g. Long-Term Viability: Prioritizing sustainable growth that supports long-term viability and profitability.

h. Competitive Advantage: Leveraging a unique value proposition and competitive advantage to capture a larger market share.

i. Risk Management: Identifying and mitigating potential risks associated with growth, such as overextending resources or losing focus.

2. Strategies for Growth and Scaling: Navigating the Expansion Journey

Growth and scaling require strategic planning and execution. Just as skilled navigators plot their course meticulously, entrepreneurs must strategize and implement growth initiatives that align with their business goals and market opportunities. Here are some key strategies for navigating the path of growth and scaling:

a. Market Expansion: Explore new geographic markets, customer segments, or product/service offerings to broaden your reach.

b. Product Diversification: Introduce new products or services that cater to the evolving needs of your customer base.

c. Strategic Partnerships: Form partnerships with complementary businesses to leverage each other's strengths and customer bases.

d. Mergers and Acquisitions: Consider acquiring or merging with other businesses to achieve rapid growth and access new markets.

e. Franchising: Scale your business by franchising, allowing others to replicate your successful model.

f. Technology Adoption: Leverage technology to streamline processes, enhance customer experience, and drive efficiency.

g. Digital Transformation: Embrace digital platforms and online channels to reach a wider audience and facilitate e-commerce.

h. Brand Building: Invest in branding and marketing efforts to increase brand visibility and attract a larger customer base.

i. Talent Acquisition: Hire skilled professionals who can drive growth initiatives and contribute to the business's expansion.

3. Innovation and Adaptation: Navigating the Changing Landscape

Innovation and adaptation serve as the compass that guides businesses through the ever-changing landscape of growth. Just as skilled navigators adjust their sails to changing winds, entrepreneurs must continuously innovate and adapt to seize new opportunities, stay relevant, and outpace competitors. Here's how to navigate the path of innovation and adaptation:

a. Customer-Centric Approach: Listen to customer feedback, anticipate their needs, and tailor your products/services accordingly.

b. Market Research: Conduct thorough market research to identify emerging trends and customer preferences.

c. Product Development: Continuously develop and improve your offerings to meet evolving customer demands.

d. Agile Methodology: Adopt agile methodologies that allow you to quickly pivot and adjust strategies based on market feedback.

e. Experimentation: Encourage a culture of experimentation, where new ideas are tested and refined.

f. Disruption: Be open to disrupting your own business model if it leads to a more innovative and competitive approach.

g. Technology Integration: Embrace emerging technologies that can enhance your products, services, or operational efficiency.

h. Continuous Learning: Invest in ongoing learning and development to stay updated on industry trends and best practices.

i. Flexibility: Maintain flexibility in your strategic planning to accommodate unexpected shifts in the market.

4. Resource Management: Navigating Efficiency and Scalability

Resource management is the compass that guides businesses in navigating the efficient allocation of resources during growth and scaling. Just as skilled navigators manage their provisions, entrepreneurs must optimize their resources to support expansion while maintaining profitability. Here's how to navigate the path of resource management:

a. Scalable Infrastructure: Build an infrastructure that can accommodate increased operational demands without compromising quality.

b. Human Capital: Invest in training, development, and talent acquisition to ensure your team is equipped to handle growth.

c. Financial Planning: Develop a solid financial plan that allocates resources effectively to support growth initiatives.

d. Technology Investment: Allocate resources to adopt technologies that enhance productivity, customer experience, and scalability.

e. Process Optimization: Streamline processes to eliminate inefficiencies and maximize the use of available resources.

f. Inventory Management: Optimize inventory levels to prevent overstocking or shortages during periods of growth.

g. Outsourcing and Partnerships: Consider outsourcing non-core functions or forming partnerships to leverage external expertise.

h. Risk Mitigation: Identify potential resource bottlenecks or shortages and have contingency plans in place.

i. Data-Driven Decision-Making: Utilize data analytics to make informed decisions about resource allocation and growth strategies.

5. Scalable Business Model: Navigating Expansion Without Strain

A scalable business model is a compass that guides businesses in expanding their operations without undue strain on resources or operations. Just as skilled navigators ensure their vessels can handle rough waters, entrepreneurs must design their business models to accommodate growth without sacrificing quality or customer satisfaction. Here's how to navigate the path of a scalable business model:

a. Standardized Processes: Develop standardized processes that can be replicated and scaled without loss of quality.

b. Automated Workflows: Implement automation to reduce manual intervention and increase operational efficiency.

c. Cloud Infrastructure: Leverage cloud-based technologies to scale IT infrastructure without large upfront investments.

d. Customer Self-Service: Offer self-service options to customers, reducing the need for additional customer support staff.

e. Flexible Pricing: Adopt pricing strategies that can adjust to changing demand and market conditions.

f. Modular Offerings: Design products or services with modular components that can be easily adapted or expanded.

g. Virtual Teams: Embrace remote work and virtual teams to tap into a broader talent pool and scale your workforce.

h. Scalable Marketing: Implement digital marketing strategies that can reach a larger audience without linear increases in costs.

i. Feedback Loop: Maintain an open feedback loop with customers to continuously improve your offerings.

6. Financial Planning: Navigating Growth's Financial Seas

Financial planning is the compass that guides businesses in navigating the financial implications of growth and scaling. Just as skilled navigators prepare financially for their journey, entrepreneurs must plan for the increased costs, investment needs, and revenue expectations that come with expansion. Here's how to navigate the path of financial planning during growth:

a. Growth Projections: Develop realistic growth projections that consider increased revenue, expenses, and profitability.

b. Investment Analysis: Assess the capital investments required to support growth initiatives and expansion.

c. Cash Flow Management: Monitor and manage cash flow to ensure you have the necessary liquidity to fund growth.

d. Financing Options: Explore financing options such as loans, lines of credit, or equity investment to support expansion.

e. Cost Structure: Analyze and optimize your cost structure to ensure that increased expenses align with revenue growth.

f. Working Capital: Ensure you have sufficient working capital to cover operational needs during periods of growth.

g. Financial Controls: Implement financial controls and reporting mechanisms to track performance against growth targets.

h. ROI Analysis: Conduct return on investment (ROI) analysis for growth initiatives to ensure they are financially viable.

i. Risk Assessment: Identify financial risks associated with growth and develop strategies to mitigate them.

7. Customer-Centric Approach: Navigating Loyalty and Retention

A customer-centric approach is the compass that guides businesses in navigating customer loyalty and retention during growth and scaling. Just as skilled navigators prioritize the safety and satisfaction of their passengers, entrepreneurs must prioritize their customers to ensure they remain loyal and engaged as the business expands. Here's how to navigate the path of a customer-centric approach during growth:

a. Customer Feedback: Continuously gather feedback from customers to understand their evolving needs and preferences.

b. Personalization: Offer personalized experiences and solutions that cater to individual customer requirements.

c. Relationship Building: Invest in building strong relationships with customers to foster loyalty and repeat business.

d. Quality Assurance: Maintain high product and service quality to ensure customer satisfaction remains consistent.

e. Communication: Keep customers informed about changes, upgrades, and expansion plans to maintain transparency.

f. Loyalty Programs: Implement loyalty programs and incentives to reward repeat customers and encourage retention.

g. Customer Support: Scale your customer support capabilities to ensure timely assistance and issue resolution.

h. Customer Journey Mapping: Understand the customer journey and identify opportunities to enhance their experience.

i. Customer Advocacy: Encourage satisfied customers to become brand advocates and refer new customers.

Navigating the Journey of Growth and Scaling

Growth and scaling represent a dynamic and transformative phase in the entrepreneurial journey, demanding strategic planning, calculated risks, and a customer-centric approach. Just as skilled navigators adapt to changing conditions and navigate uncharted waters, entrepreneurs must anticipate challenges, seize opportunities, and make informed decisions to navigate the journey of growth successfully.

By understanding the strategies for growth, embracing innovation, optimizing resources, designing scalable business models, planning financially, and adopting a customer-centric approach, entrepreneurs can steer their businesses toward expanded horizons and sustainable success. Just as the legacy of skilled navigators lives on in the stories of their journeys, the legacy of entrepreneurs lives on in the impact of their businesses on markets, industries, and communities—forging a path toward enduring success and prosperity.

CHAPTER FOURTEEN
Networking and Partnerships

In the vast expanse of the business landscape, networking and partnerships serve as the compass that guides entrepreneurs toward a world of opportunities, collaborations, and growth.

Just as skilled navigators build alliances to navigate treacherous waters, entrepreneurs must harness the power of networking and partnerships to navigate the complexities of modern business.

This exploration delves into the multifaceted realm of networking and partnerships, unveiling the strategies that underpin successful relationship-building, collaboration, and long-term business success.

1. Understanding Networking and Partnerships: The Fabric of Business Connectivity

Networking and partnerships are not mere social interactions; they are the threads that weave together the fabric of business connectivity. Networking involves building and nurturing relationships with individuals and organizations within your industry or related fields.

Partnerships, on the other hand, are formal collaborations between entities to achieve shared goals. Here's a closer look at the key components of networking and partnerships:

a. Relationship Building: Establishing genuine connections with people who can offer support, advice, and opportunities.

b. Collaboration: Joining forces with other entities to leverage each other's strengths and resources.

c. Knowledge Sharing: Exchanging insights, expertise, and information to collectively enhance understanding and innovation.

d. Market Expansion: Leveraging the networks and customer bases of partners to access new markets.

e. Skill Enrichment: Learning from others' experiences, skills, and perspectives to enhance personal and professional growth.

f. Resource Access: Tapping into partners' resources, whether financial, intellectual, or operational, to achieve common goals.

g. Risk Mitigation: Spreading risks and challenges by sharing responsibilities and collaborating on problem-solving.

h. Innovation: Fostering a collaborative environment that sparks innovation through diverse viewpoints and expertise.

i. Win-Win Dynamics: Establishing partnerships that benefit all parties involved by creating mutually advantageous outcomes.

2. Strategies for Effective Networking: Navigating the Web of Relationships

Networking is a skill that requires deliberate effort and strategic planning. Just as skilled navigators chart their course to avoid obstacles, entrepreneurs must navigate the web of relationships by developing effective networking strategies. Here are some key strategies for navigating the path of effective networking:

a. Identify Goals: Define clear goals for networking, whether it's expanding your customer base, seeking mentorship, or finding business partners.

b. Targeted Events: Attend industry conferences, seminars, workshops, and networking events that align with your goals.

c. Online Platforms: Utilize social media, professional networking platforms, and forums to connect with a wider audience.

d. Elevator Pitch: Craft a concise and compelling elevator pitch that effectively communicates who you are and what you do.

e. Active Listening: Practice active listening to understand others' needs and how you can provide value.

f. Follow-Up: After initial interactions, follow up with connections through personalized messages to strengthen relationships.

g. Networking Groups: Join industry-specific or interest-based networking groups to connect with like-minded individuals.

h. Value Exchange: Offer value to your connections by sharing insights, resources, or referrals that can benefit them.

i. Long-Term Relationship: Focus on building long-term relationships rather than just seeking immediate gains.

3. Collaborative Partnerships: Navigating the Journey Together

Collaborative partnerships are the compass that guides businesses toward shared success and mutual growth.

Just as skilled navigators form alliances for joint expeditions, entrepreneurs must identify and cultivate partnerships that align with their goals and values. Here's how to navigate the path of collaborative partnerships:

a. Shared Vision: Seek partners who share a common vision, mission, and values to ensure alignment.

b. Complementary Skills: Choose partners who bring complementary skills and expertise to the table.

c. Clear Roles: Define clear roles and responsibilities for each partner to avoid conflicts and confusion.

d. Open Communication: Maintain open and transparent communication to ensure all partners are on the same page.

e. Mutually Beneficial: Design partnerships that offer value to all parties involved, leading to mutual benefit.

f. Legal Agreements: Draft formal agreements that outline expectations, contributions, and terms of the partnership.

g. Consensus Decision-Making: Make decisions collaboratively, involving all partners in the decision-making process.

h. Flexibility: Be adaptable and open to adjustments as the partnership evolves and market conditions change.

i. Conflict Resolution: Establish mechanisms for resolving conflicts and disagreements in a constructive manner.

4. Cross-Industry Collaboration: Navigating Uncharted Territories

Cross-industry collaboration is the compass that guides businesses into uncharted territories, unlocking new avenues for innovation and growth. Just as skilled navigators explore new routes, entrepreneurs must venture beyond their comfort zones to form partnerships with entities in different industries. Here's how to navigate the path of cross-industry collaboration:

a. Identify Synergies: Explore industries with synergies that align with your business's products, services, or values.

b. Innovative Solutions: Combine expertise from different industries to develop innovative solutions and products.

c. Open-Mindedness: Approach cross-industry collaboration with an open mind and a willingness to learn.

d. Market Insights: Gain insights into customer behaviors and preferences from industries different from your own.

e. New Customer Segments: Access new customer segments that were previously untapped by your business.

f. Shared Resources: Share resources, research, and capabilities with partners from different industries.

g. Risk Sharing: Spread risks by diversifying into industries that may have different cycles and market dynamics.

h. Regulatory Expertise: Learn from partners in industries with different regulatory environments and compliance standards.

i. Creative Thinking: Encourage creative thinking and brainstorming sessions to uncover innovative possibilities.

5. Strategic Alliances: Navigating Mutual Growth

Strategic alliances are the compass that guides businesses toward mutual growth and shared success. Just as skilled navigators team up for collaborative exploration, entrepreneurs must strategically align with other entities to achieve common goals. Here's how to navigate the path of strategic alliances:

a. Common Goals: Partner with entities that share similar long-term objectives and aspirations.

b. Complementary Strengths: Identify partners with strengths that complement your business's weaknesses.

c. Market Access: Gain access to new markets, customer bases, or distribution channels through your alliance.

d. Joint Marketing: Collaborate on marketing campaigns, promotions, and initiatives to enhance visibility.

e. Resource Pooling: Pool resources, whether financial, intellectual, or operational, to achieve shared goals.

f. Co-Creation: Jointly create products, services, or solutions that leverage each partner's expertise.

g. Risk Management: Share risks associated with new ventures or market entries by leveraging combined strengths.

h. Continuous Evaluation: Regularly evaluate the alliance's progress and effectiveness toward achieving objectives.

i. Long-Term Planning: Develop a clear long-term plan for the alliance, including growth targets and exit strategies.

6. Global Networking: Navigating International Markets

Global networking is the compass that guides businesses into international markets, connecting entrepreneurs with opportunities across borders. Just as skilled navigators venture into international waters, entrepreneurs must expand their networks beyond their local communities to access a global arena. Here's how to navigate the path of global networking:

a. Cultural Sensitivity: Embrace cultural diversity and practice sensitivity when interacting with international contacts.

b. Language Proficiency: Learn key languages or work with translators to effectively communicate with international partners.

c. International Events: Attend international conferences, trade shows, and expos to connect with a diverse range of professionals.

d. Virtual Connections: Leverage digital platforms to connect with professionals and businesses from around the world.

e. Local Partnerships: Form partnerships with local businesses in foreign markets to gain insights and access.

f. Regulatory Knowledge: Familiarize yourself with international regulations and compliance standards when entering new markets.

g. Time Zone Management: Coordinate effectively with partners in different time zones to facilitate communication and collaboration.

h. Adaptability: Be adaptable and open to adjusting strategies based on the nuances of different international markets.

i. Global Mindset: Develop a global mindset that allows you to navigate cultural, economic, and social differences.

Navigating the Tapestry of Connections

Networking and partnerships are not just transactions; they are the intricate tapestry of connections that shape the landscape of modern business.

Just as skilled navigators rely on alliances to navigate uncharted waters, entrepreneurs must forge meaningful relationships, collaborate strategically, and expand their networks to steer their businesses toward success.

By understanding the strategies for effective networking, cultivating collaborative partnerships, exploring cross-industry collaborations, forming strategic alliances, engaging in global networking, and embracing a customer-centric approach, entrepreneurs can navigate the complexities of the business world with finesse.

Just as the legacy of skilled navigators lives on in the stories of their journeys, the legacy of entrepreneurs lives on in the connections they nurture, the partnerships they foster, and the impact they create—crafting a path toward enduring prosperity and innovation.

CHAPTER FIFTEEN
Stay Persistent and Resilient

In the vast expanse of the entrepreneurial journey, persistence and resilience serve as the compass that guides individuals through storms, setbacks, and uncertainties.

Just as skilled navigators weather turbulent waters with unwavering determination, entrepreneurs must harness the power of persistence and resilience to navigate challenges, overcome obstacles, and achieve their goals.

This exploration delves into the multifaceted world of staying persistent and resilient, unveiling the strategies that underpin steadfast determination, adaptive thinking, and long-term success.

1. Understanding Persistence and Resilience: The Pillars of Entrepreneurial Fortitude

Persistence and resilience are not mere traits; they are the pillars of entrepreneurial fortitude that enable individuals to overcome adversity and forge ahead.

Persistence involves steadfastly pursuing goals despite obstacles and failures, while resilience entails bouncing back from setbacks, adapting to change, and thriving in the face of adversity. Here's a closer look at the key components of persistence and resilience:

a.   Determination: Exhibiting unyielding determination to achieve long-term goals, regardless of challenges.

b. Grit: Demonstrating grit by maintaining passion and perseverance in the pursuit of objectives.

c.   Adaptability: Adapting to changing circumstances and making adjustments as needed.

d. Emotional Strength: Developing emotional strength to cope with stress, uncertainty, and disappointments.

e. Problem-solving: Navigating obstacles by approaching problems with creative and innovative solutions.

f. Endurance: Building endurance to withstand setbacks, failures, and prolonged challenges.

g. Learning Mindset: Embracing a mindset of continuous learning and growth from both successes and failures.

h. Optimism: Cultivating optimism and a positive outlook even in the face of adversity.

i. Goal Orientation: Maintaining a clear focus on long-term goals while managing short-term setbacks.

2. Strategies for Staying Persistent: Navigating the Path of Tenacity

Staying persistent requires deliberate effort and strategic thinking. Just as skilled navigators steer their vessels through difficult waters, entrepreneurs must navigate the path of tenacity by employing effective strategies. Here are some key strategies for staying persistent in the face of challenges:

a. Clear Goals: Define clear and meaningful goals that provide a sense of purpose and direction.

b. Break Down Tasks: Break down complex challenges into smaller, manageable tasks to maintain a sense of progress.

c. Positive Self-Talk: Practice positive self-talk and affirmations to reinforce determination and motivation.

d. Daily Routine: Establish a structured daily routine that includes focused work toward your goals.

e. Visualize Success: Visualize your desired outcomes and success regularly to maintain motivation.

f. Accountability: Share your goals with a trusted friend, mentor, or coach who can hold you accountable.

g. Learn from Setbacks: View setbacks as opportunities to learn and grow, rather than as failures.

h. Embrace Failure: Embrace failure as an integral part of the journey and a stepping stone toward success.

i. Celebrate Progress: Celebrate even small victories along the way to stay motivated and acknowledge your efforts.

3. Embracing Resilience: Navigating Bounce-Back Ability

Embracing resilience is the compass that guides entrepreneurs through turbulent times, allowing them to bounce back stronger from challenges. Just as skilled navigators repair their vessels and resume their journeys, entrepreneurs must cultivate the ability to bounce back and thrive after setbacks. Here's how to navigate the path of resilience:

a. Mindfulness: Practice mindfulness and self-awareness to manage stress and build emotional resilience.

b. Positive Mindset: Foster a positive mindset by focusing on solutions and opportunities rather than problems.

c. Acceptance: Accept that change and challenges are a natural part of the entrepreneurial journey.

d. Seek Support: Reach out to friends, family, mentors, or support groups during tough times.

e. Learn from Adversity: Reflect on challenges to extract valuable lessons that contribute to personal growth.

f. Flexibility: Cultivate flexibility to adapt to unexpected changes and make necessary adjustments.

g. Manage Stress: Develop stress-management techniques such as exercise, meditation, or deep breathing.

h. Emotional Intelligence: Enhance emotional intelligence to manage emotions and navigate difficult conversations.

i. Forward-Thinking: Focus on the future and the opportunities that lie ahead, rather than dwelling on setbacks.

4. Resilient Decision-Making: Navigating Uncertainty with Confidence

Resilient decision-making is the compass that guides entrepreneurs in navigating uncertainty with confidence. Just as skilled navigators make informed decisions amid unpredictable weather, entrepreneurs must make choices that reflect adaptability, resourcefulness, and calculated risk-taking. Here's how to navigate the path of resilient decision-making:

a. Risk Assessment: Evaluate risks and benefits thoroughly before making decisions.

b. Scenario Planning: Anticipate potential outcomes and develop contingency plans for different scenarios.

c. Data-Informed: Base decisions on accurate data and insights, rather than on impulse or emotion.

d. Seek Expert Advice: Consult with mentors, advisors, or experts in relevant fields to gain perspectives.

e. Trust Intuition: Listen to your gut instincts, especially when faced with ambiguous situations.

f. Iterate and Adapt: Be open to iterating decisions based on new information or changing circumstances.

g. Long-Term Vision: Consider the long-term implications of decisions, beyond short-term gains.

h. Failure Preparedness: Make decisions with an understanding that some may not yield the desired results, and be prepared to adapt accordingly.

i. Reflect and Learn: Reflect on the outcomes of your decisions, both positive and negative, to refine your decision-making process.

5. Mental and Emotional Resilience: Navigating Inner Strength

Mental and emotional resilience is the compass that guides entrepreneurs in cultivating inner strength to overcome challenges. Just as skilled navigators draw upon their inner resources during tough times, entrepreneurs must develop strategies to maintain mental and emotional well-being. Here's how to navigate the path of mental and emotional resilience:

a. Self-Care: Prioritize self-care through exercise, proper nutrition, sleep, and relaxation.

b. Mindset Shift: Reframe challenges as opportunities for growth and learning.

c. Practice Gratitude: Cultivate gratitude by focusing on the positive aspects of your journey.

d. Limit Negative Inputs: Minimize exposure to negative news, people, or environments that drain your energy.

e. Social Connections: Maintain a supportive network of friends, family, mentors, and peers.

f. Seek Professional Help: If needed, seek the assistance of mental health professionals to manage stress and challenges.

g. Creative Outlets: Engage in creative hobbies or activities that provide a sense of accomplishment and relaxation.

h. Stress Reduction: Use stress reduction techniques such as mindfulness, meditation, or journaling.

i. Emotional Expression: Allow yourself to express your emotions in a healthy and constructive manner.

6. Turning Adversity into Opportunity: Navigating Transformation

Turning adversity into opportunity is the compass that guides entrepreneurs to transform challenges into catalysts for growth.

Just as skilled navigators find new routes amid obstacles, entrepreneurs must leverage setbacks to pivot, innovate, and evolve. Here's how to navigate the path of turning adversity into opportunity:

a. Shift Perspective: Change your perspective by viewing challenges as opportunities for innovation and improvement.

b. Problem-Solving: Channel your energy into finding creative solutions to the challenges you face.

c. Pivot Strategies: If circumstances change, be open to pivoting your strategies and adjusting your approach.

d. Continuous Learning: Embrace a mindset of continuous learning, seeking insights from both successes and failures.

e. Customer Feedback: Use customer feedback and market insights to adapt your products or services.

f. Agility: Develop agility by remaining flexible and open to new ideas and approaches.

g. Experimentation: Experiment with new approaches, products, or markets to discover untapped potential.

h. Resilient Leadership: Demonstrate resilient leadership by remaining calm, focused, and optimistic during tough times.

i. Seize Opportunities: Actively seek out opportunities that arise from challenges and disruptions.

Navigating Challenges with Unwavering Resolve

Staying persistent and resilient is not just a survival tactic; it's a transformative approach that empowers entrepreneurs to navigate challenges with unwavering resolve.

Just as skilled navigators steer their vessels through rough waters, entrepreneurs must harness their inner strength, adaptability, and determination to navigate the unpredictable terrain of business.

By understanding the strategies for staying persistent, embracing resilience, making resilient decisions, cultivating mental and emotional well-being, turning adversity into opportunity, and leading with resolve, entrepreneurs can navigate challenges as opportunities for growth and innovation.

Just as the legacy of skilled navigators lives on in the tales of their journeys, the legacy of entrepreneurs lives on in the impact they create, the innovations they bring forth, and the stories of triumph they inspire—forging a path toward enduring success and fulfillment.